# workplace
## warrior

# workplace warrior

Insights and Advice

for Winning on the

Corporate Battlefield

KAY HAMMER

AMACOM

**American Management Association**
New York • Atlanta • Boston • Chicago • Kansas City • San Francisco • Washington, D.C.
Brussels • Mexico City • Tokyo • Toronto

Special discount on bulk quantities of AMACOM books are
available to corporations, professional associations, and
other organizations. For details, contact Special Sales Department,
AMACOM, an imprint of AMA Publications, a division of
American Management Association, 1601 Broadway,
New York, NY 10019. Tel: 212-903-8316. Fax: 212-903-8083.

This publication is designed to provide accurate and authoritative information in regard to the subject matter covered. It is sold with the understanding that the publisher is not engaged in rendering legal, accounting, or
other professional service. If legal advice or other expert assistance is
required, the services of a competent professional person should be sought.

Permissions information is to be found on pg. xiv.

Library of Congress Cataloging-in-Publication Data

Hammer, Kay.
     Workplace warrior: insights and advice for winning on the corpo-
     rate battlefield/Kay Hammer.
        p. cm.
     Includes bibliographical references and index.
     ISBN 0-8144-0494-4
     1. Hammer, Kay. 2. Women executives—United States—
     Biography. I. Title.

HD6054.2.U6H35 2000
650.1'082—dc21
                                 00-025280

Printing number
10 9 8 7 6 5 4 3 2 1

*To Kat and Evie*

# contents

# preface

*In our scriptures, it is said that there are four kinds of horses: excellent ones, good ones, poor ones, and bad ones. The best horse will run slow and fast, right and left, at the driver's will, before it sees the shadow of a whip; the second best will run as well as the first one, just before the whip reaches the skin; the third one will run when it feels pain on its body; the fourth one will run after the pain penetrates to the marrow of its bones. . .*

*When we hear this story, almost all of us want to be the best horse. If it is impossible to be the best one, we want to be the second best. . . . But those who find great difficulties in practicing Zen will find more meaning in it. So sometimes I think that the best horse may be the worst horse, and the worst horse can be the best one.*

—SHUNRYU SUZUKI,
*Zen Mind, Beginner's Mind* [1]

Most of the insights I have gained into how to succeed in the workplace came from being a "poor horse." I was naive about the way the world worked and unsure of what I wanted from it and what it would take for me to get it once I knew. Consequently, in the struggle to figure out why I was not successful or satisfied, I hit on a number of self-limiting misconceptions that I believe most people share. The purpose of this book is to articulate these misconceptions and to discuss the effective and, equally important, ineffective means I have found for breaking free from them.

For the first two-thirds of my life, I made life-changing decisions impulsively not to achieve some goal or desire, but to escape emotionally untenable situations. At nineteen, I married my sophomore literature teacher after a six-week courtship and moved to Iowa to get away from my father and the limitations of life in Shreveport, Louisiana. After twelve years of marriage, two daughters, and two advanced degrees, I divorced my husband to escape a relationship devoid of trust and filled with betrayals.

But at thirty-one, I found myself in a position where I couldn't run away or rush headlong into a new life. I had custody of my daughters. My ex-husband, devastated by the divorce, had moved to New York to pursue his dream of an acting career. I had to assume the roles of father and provider as well as mother. Fortunately, I had completed my doctorate and, by the time of my divorce, was up for tenure at Washington State University teaching literature and linguistics in the Department of English.

I could provide my girls with a reasonably comfortable life but not make up for the emotional assault they had suffered in the divorce. But as each semester passed, I felt more trapped—not by the children, but by my dwindling sense of hope for a happier life. With double-digit inflation and single-digit raises, the thought of growing old in Pullman, a town with 16,000-plus students and approximately 12,000 residents, was grim.

Then I had an epiphany. The week before classes started in the fall of 1979, I was preparing syllabi in my office, looking out on the wheat fields of Pullman and the mountains in Idaho, when I faced the hard realization that nothing substantive would change in my life unless I made it happen. No Prince Charming was going to do it.

That day, I decided to make a conscious effort to change my life. From that day forward, though I may not have been happy with some aspects of my life, my life was my own.

The details of my plan are less important than the process. I decided that money and mobility were the two most important things I wanted in my new life, so that if I found myself feeling trapped, I could move on without worrying about meeting my obligations to the girls. I decided that a career in the computer software industry was most likely to fit my skills and offer those benefits. To move toward that goal, I obviously had to take classes, which was not so hard for someone who already made her living on a university campus. My next logical step was to apply for a sabbatical so I could study elsewhere for a year and see what it felt like to live somewhere besides Pullman. Beyond that, I had no plan, just a sense that, if I set off on this path, eventually I would be better off.

The twenty years since that epiphany have been hard, so hard at times that I felt like I was waging war. I married a decent man who disliked my older daughter, who in turn suffered a tortured adolescence. My mother died after heart surgery. Three months later, my father succumbed to a hard, slow death from a brain tumor that had destroyed his ability to speak, read, or write and so eliminated any possibility of our resolving our troubled love for each other. I divorced. My children lost their father's companion, who had been a devoted stepparent, to AIDS, and I lost one of my closest friends to lung cancer. And throughout this period, I fought constant battles at work against bosses, office politics, and even the very dynamics of the organizations in which I worked.

But mine is a happy story. I learned that conflict can bring great rewards if it is approached correctly, I learned which battles to fight and which to avoid, and I learned that success is tied to understanding your enemy, who sometimes is yourself. As I was learning these lessons, my daughters were growing into wonderful, perceptive women in whom I have great trust. Before my mother died, she and I had the opportunity to recognize and appreciate each other's strengths while dealing with my father's illness. I have experienced more professional success and satisfaction than I could ever have imagined. I am even beginning to develop a capacity for joy.

Also important, I have learned how and why war is a good metaphor for life:

■ If you take responsibility for your life, you will be required to put yourself at risk. With risk comes fear and with fear the need to face the demons of your childhood. We all have demons from our childhood; it's the human condition.

■ Life, like war, calls for a strategy, but just as a battle plan must constantly be adjusted to accommodate what actually happens on the battlefield, you must be prepared to amend your plans in life to accommodate changing conditions.

■ Finally, in war those who persevere in the face of defeat emerge victorious. A strong warrior trains himself to fight on in spite of pain, fear, and uncertainty and to learn from defeat.[2] In life, we must do the same.

This story, then, is of one poor horse. What follows is the marrow of the lessons she has learned.

## Note to the Reader

This book describes a wide variety of lessons I have learned over a period of twenty years in business. If you are an entrepreneur or want to start a company, then Section I, Rules of Engagement, will be of interest. In this section, I consider the issues involved with starting and growing a private company and how this differs from running a public company. In addition, I discuss the pros and cons of choosing to take a company public versus selling it or merging with another entity. On the other hand, if you already know or are less concerned with issues of company finance and governance and want to become more comfortable in dealing with conflict, you may choose to skip that section and go on to Section II. In this section, Basic Training, I consider the issues and analytical skills that help determine who are allies and who are enemies (sometimes it's a question of where *you* fall). I also look at the best methods of confronting conflict and gathering support. Section III, The Battle and Beyond, focuses on guidelines you should use once you have decided to "go to war," and looks at the issue of defeat and how we deal with it.

## Notes

1. Shunryu Suzuki, *Zen Mind, Beginner's Mind* (Trumbull, Conn.: Weatherhill, 1972), pp. 33–39.

2. I believe most of the topics addressed in this book apply as much to men as to women. As a result, I have opted to use *he* or *she* arbitrarily throughout.

The publisher gratefully acknowledges permission to print excerpts from the following:

*Do What You Love, The Money Will Follow* by Marsha Sinetar, copyright © 1989 by Marsha Sinetar. Used by permission of Dell Publishing, a division of Random House, Inc.

"nobody loses all the time." Copyright 1926, 1954, © 1991 by the Trustees for the E. E. Cummings Trust. Copyright © 1985 by George James Firmage, from Complete Poems: 1904-1962 by E. E. Cummings, edited George J. Firmage. Used by Permission of Liveright Publishing Corporation.

# acknowledgments

I would like to thank Robin Curle, my cofounder of ETI and my coach through my early days in business, and Bob Inman, our first investor who is a wonderful mentor and model of wisdom, humanity, and integrity. In addition, the support of George Kozmetsky and Les Belady has been invaluable, as well as the help of many others, including Gene Lowenthal, Tom Kirkland, Frank Peters, and John Jarve. Thanks also to my assistant and friend Rebecca Foletta and my good friend Shahriar Ghaffari for their support and efforts in helping me in the process of writing this book. Then there are all my colleagues at ETI, including David Marshall, Gérard Simon, and Fiona McInally, who have tolerated my learning curve while helping us move the company forward.

Finally, there would be no book without the efforts of Karl Weber, my agent, and all the super people at AMACOM—Ellen Kadin, Andy Ambraziejus, Cathleen Ouderkirk, and Kama Timbrell. Thank you, all.

# The Need to Take Arms
## Three Levels of Professional Maturation

**W**hen I was a junior at the University of Iowa, I took a Bible as Literature course taught by a compelling professor named Nancy Andreasen. On the last day of class, she told us that she had particularly bitter-sweet feelings about the end of the semester because it was the last time she would be teaching in the Department of English. She was quitting the faculty to attend medical school.

More than twenty years later, while reading the *Austin American-Statesman,* I came upon a short article describing the work of a psychiatrist named Nancy Andreasen, whose research had demonstrated a higher incidence of emotional disorders among people with professions in the arts than in the general population. Intrigued, I called her office—she was still at the University of Iowa—and her secretary forwarded me a couple of her journal articles. One study focused on her work with writers enrolled at the Iowa Writers' Workshop, one of the country's earliest and most successful creative writing programs.

Based on this reading, and remembering how many of the greatest American novelists have been alcoholics, I found myself wondering which comes first—the pursuit of a creative career or the affective/addictive disorders? Perhaps it is neither. Perhaps what drives some people to both drink and write is that they see too clearly what others choose to ignore. Too often, the root of people's heartache lies not in their circumstances—abandoned by a parent or unappreciated by a boss or spouse—but in their failure to acknowledge their pain. Perhaps the writer's pain comes from his inability to make others see what he sees, or to make them acknowledge his reality. Thus, writers might write to bear witness to their vision and drink to escape it.

It's not just writers who are hurt when others do not acknowledge their perceptions of reality. Most of our emotional discomfort that is not immediately tied to grief or physical pain can be seen as the result of conflicts in perception—and too often the perception of *all* parties involved needs readjustment.

How are pain and the ability to acknowledge pain related to our lives at work? Pain and its lesser offspring, dissatisfaction and discomfort, can be great teachers if we learn to attend to them directly rather than seeking to escape or deny them. For much of my life, whenever I felt depressed or unhappy, I attributed it either to some shortcoming in myself or to some bad stroke of luck. In response, I would take some dramatic action to change my situation, such as agreeing to marry someone after having dated him for only seven days and then going through with it six weeks later. It certainly distracted me. What with moving to Iowa, going to school, having babies, and so on, twelve years passed before I felt sufficiently miserable to make another dramatic shift, this time in the direction of divorce. What I *hadn't* done was look hard at why I was unhappy and take action to change myself as well as my circumstances.

Until finally I did. As a divorced mother of two, I wished that someone would appear on the horizon who would make my life all better; most women want to believe in Prince Charming. But with my analytical bent, I realized that the odds of this rescue happening were not in my favor. And the thought of becoming a faded academic unable to provide my children with the life I felt they deserved was unbearable. After months of depression, I finally decided to stop hoping for something to change, to face what hurt, and to do what I could to improve what I didn't like. You can't will yourself to be lovable or loved (at least, I didn't think so at the time), but you can change your professional life. I decided to start there.

Since that time, I have probably experienced the same amount of pain and heartache as before, but with one difference. Now I see pain as a sign that I am not attending to something. *The body never lies; it just doesn't speak in English.* Feelings are among our most important resources, that is, if we acknowledge them and do something about them. Hatred or anger is a sign that there are two battles to fight—an internal one as well as an external one. If you fail to face and fight the internal battle, regardless of the external battle's outcome, one day you will have to fight the same battle again.

In my case, it wasn't until I realized I still held deep resentment about my father's arbitrary and authoritarian manner that I understood why I kept picking bosses who behaved similarly. It was as if by going to battle with them, I could finally beat Daddy. Looking back, it surprises me how long it took me to face what was bothering me at different junctures in my life. In the end, however, I have always been deeply relieved after I've faced some particular demon and moved on. It seems to me that there were two causes for my delays—my level of maturity and my imperfect understanding of the growth process.

## Three Stages of Personal and Professional Growth

After more than eighteen years of business experience and a considerable amount of sometimes painful reflection, I have concluded that there are three levels of professional maturation. All three can be characterized by their attitudes toward risk and the need for approval. These three stages are those of the apprentice, the warrior, and the adventurer.

With few exceptions, most of us have to master one stage before we can proceed to the next. One skill required for any transition is the ability to recognize when your dissatisfaction or pain is not simply an outgrowth of some particular conflict but rather signals a need for personal growth. In some respects, then, pain can serve as the midwife of a newer self, struggling to be born.

## Stage One: The Apprentice

Most of us start in the workplace as apprentices, a natural outgrowth of our earlier roles as child and student. The defining characteristic of the apprentice is the need for external approval. Just as a child craves approval from a parent, the apprentice is eager for her supervisor and others in the chain of command to recognize her commitment, talent, and achievement. Thus, the apprentice is always looking for signs. A nod in the hall, or its absence, or the tone of some small talk after a meeting is stored away as evidence that the boss thinks she is doing well or poorly.

Because they are so concerned with external judgment, ambitious apprentices are frequently their own worst critics. They strive not merely to improve their work but to achieve an elusive level of quality they identify with perfection. Even if their work is regularly judged as superior, apprentices seem to need permission to take the next step. Hence, they constantly search for some sign that they should seek a promotion or the chance to tackle a special project.

If apprentices do not get sufficient recognition for their efforts, they can become frustrated or bitter. Frustration need not be bad; it can often be the impetus for an apprentice growing into the role of a warrior. But bitterness is a poison that, if allowed to accumulate, can ruin not only your career but your personal life as well.

## Common Misconceptions by the Apprentice
Apprentices often fail to get the recognition they desire because of invalid assumptions they hold about the workplace. Let's consider some of these false and dangerous beliefs and the underlying realities.

*"Good work is its own advertisement."* Conventional wisdom says that we are judged by our deeds rather than our words, and as children, we are taught that humility is a virtue. But too often, in an attempt to let their efforts speak for themselves, employees—and perhaps especially women—expect their managers to accurately assess their achievements without their having to articulate them. This expectation is unrealistic.

Sometimes the manager's workload is to blame. For example, it may be reasonable to expect a software development manager to perform a detailed review of each programmer's specifications for a project, but it's unrealistic to think that he will review all of the code written by each individual. Instead, the manager relies on external evidence of achievement, such as whether the individual's code is completed on schedule and is found free of faults during the test cycle. While these measures are a good rule of thumb, they can often be manipulated by less conscientious employees to the detriment of their more conscientious coworkers.

Consider the case of J, who worked as a systems programmer at a hardware manufacturer. Relatively new out of school, J was delighted when assigned the task of designing and implementing a Pascal compiler. Eager to do an excellent job, J took a fair amount of time researching and revising his initial design and was always extremely conservative in reporting his progress.

In the software development field, projects frequently

experience "fire drills," or emergency situations where extra effort is required to meet a release schedule. On numerous occasions during the first six months of his Pascal project, J's boss, Mr. M, assigned J to help out with other projects that were under intense deadline pressure. J assumed that his boss knew these additional assignments would affect J's ability to deliver the Pascal compiler on time; however, Mr. M wasn't aware of the adverse impact on J's schedule, probably because he himself was juggling the schedules for five or six projects.

As the original release date for the compiler approached, Mr. M, who had not prepared *his* boss for the need to slip the compiler's availability date, became annoyed at J for not keeping him informed of the delays. In order to hold as close to the original date as possible, Mr. M brought R to assist the project.

R had worked for the company for more than five years and was an excellent systems programmer, but he had become very cynical about his career and spent considerable time during work hours on personal activities, organizing softball leagues and planning ski trips. With R's help—and some late nights and weekends, J managed to release the compiler close to the original date promised, primarily because J had done a good job with the original design and was almost finished with the implementation when R was assigned to the project. However, Mr. M praised R and gave him the higher raise that year, even though J had actually been the more valuable employee.

The moral here is never assume that your managers are aware of the quality of your work. Your job is to apprise them of your progress, both good and bad. Learning to articulate what you have done well is what most bosses would consider proper humility and is every bit as important as listing your failings.

**"I may not be good enough to succeed at a first-rate company, so it would be better to remain here where I'm sure to succeed."**
Conscientious people are self-critical. Just as this trait often con-

tributes to reticence about singing one's own praises, it also keeps people from aiming as high as they should.

Whether it was because I didn't get to attend the Ivy League college I had had my heart set on or because, when I landed at the University of Iowa, I quickly realized how culturally limited my lower-middle-class upbringing in Louisiana had been, I spent a good part of my early professional life feeling second-rate. I was always perceived as a bright and successful student or employee, but underneath my self-confident surface, I was always afraid of revealing my limitations.

As a result, I wouldn't apply for special programs or attempt to achieve recognition except by dutifully fulfilling the requirements of my job. I always felt I needed to prove myself, thus I would seek to establish myself in a less competitive setting first, thinking that once I received recognition that it would be clear that I was worthy to try for something more ambitious.

I've since learned this assumption is commonplace and shared by many people studying or working in organizations that are not at the top of their field. Simple arithmetic tells you that, in any field, the great majority of organizations are second-rate; everyone can't be number one. The big problem is, too often, the people supervising you in a second-string environment suffer from the same feelings of inadequacy you have. They make poor managers because they too are locked in to their own need for external judgment and approval. If you wait for them to encourage and support you, you may wait forever.

Once I finally allowed myself to compete in first-string environments, I found successful people are frequently the most generous and effective managers, because they feel secure about themselves. Consequently, before you write yourself off as unready to take on some challenge and settle for something that you feel is second best, think about how the need for and fear of judgment may be paralyzing you. As long as you approach your work conscientiously and learn to be honest about your shortcomings and your successes, you can be an asset to any organization regardless of its stature or prestige. And if you do find yourself in over your head, don't despair. Examine your limitations to see what you can improve and apply yourself to doing that, even if it means changing jobs or companies. If you do, you will retain the respect of your colleagues and management.

*"All I need is a mentor."* Just as we looked for guidance and approval from our parents when we were children, most of us long for guidance and approval from a mentor in our professional lives. We imagine working with someone who, recognizing our talents, can help us overcome our weaknesses and give us encouragement when we are ready to "go for it." Unfortunately, this expectation is usually unrealistic.

There are two types of mentors: those who mentor to fulfill some unmet need in themselves and those who mentor to give back to the community that has nurtured and rewarded them. At different stages of development, an individual can be both types of mentor. The type of mentor one acquires at the apprentice stage, however, is often the person who is mentoring to fulfill his own needs.

Extremely successful people are busy and passionately engaged with their own challenges. While they are frequently generous with their advice and time, they are usually partnering with their peers—other people already engaged in significant pursuits at a high professional level. You cannot expect someone whose schedule is booked a year in advance to take the time first to look over your shoulder and notice that you are talented and then to convince you that you are ready to advance. If you do manage to attract the attention of a top-level leader, he may compliment you or give you an introduction, but your ability to advance will depend on your assuming new challenges without waiting for encouragement or reassurance.

The kind of mentor who will give such personal reassurance to an apprentice is more likely one who is performing this service as much for her own needs as to help you. Consequently, because the mentor has a hidden agenda, you will usually find that you ultimately have to abandon the relationship to mature. This leave-taking is frequently painful and can irreparably damage the relationship.

I personally have mentored two younger women since I entered the business world. Part of my motivation in doing so was out of respect for their intellect and the joy I experienced in working with them, but in part I tried to make up for the fact that at the time my older daughter and I were alienated. Being a good mother has always been extremely important to me, and I felt that, in the case of my older daughter, I had failed. So I found myself wanting the two young women I mentored not just to respect me but to love me.

In both cases, each of these young women eventually became sufficiently secure in her skills and aware enough of my limitations to leave the relationship. T, with whom I had worked closely for four years, accepted a job offer from another company. She talked frankly with me about being ready to step out in a lead position rather than serving as my second in command. Although she didn't feel the need to speak critically of what she saw as my limitations, I was aware of T's opinions and felt some resentment. We both behaved professionally, however, and today, we are once again colleagues. Although we have not resumed the intense personal relationship we once had, we do respect and like each other.

The other case did not turn out so well. When S became frustrated in her career and ready to move on, she attempted to unseat me. Well-armed with a knowledge of my weaknesses, which I would have revealed only to someone I trusted, and encouraged by her husband, she went to war with me—and lost. I won the battle with S, but my heart was broken in the process. Although I continue to mentor people, I will never give so freely of myself to anyone again. This change is probably very healthy and a lesson I needed to learn.

Bear two things in mind about mentors. First, because they share their experience and wisdom with you out of affection and respect for you, mentors frequently will temper their reprimands and soften their anger, much as loving parents do. If you choose to go to war with a mentor, be warned that you may meet a very different person on the battlefield.

Second, if you have not found a mentor, it is no excuse to avoid moving forward in your career. If you're waiting for an external sign of your readiness to advance, you probably aren't ready. You may need to wait until you are sufficiently desperate for change to proceed without encouragement.

## Trapped in Apprenticeship

Some people are content to stay in the role of apprentice indefinitely and are satisfied in serving their company as individual contributors throughout their careers. These individuals usually take pleasure in their day-to-day work—whether it's keeping a set of books, teaching an English class, or drafting engineering diagrams—and get enough financial and emotional rewards from their companies to feel appreciated. But those who are more ambitious eventually want more responsibility. If they do not get it, they will either become coffee-room cynics or make the transition to warrior.

Those who are unready to make the transition, those trapped in apprenticeship, are typically afraid of overt conflict and prefer rationalizing their unhappiness rather than doing open battle with themselves or others. Let's consider the kinds of rationalizations these people use and why these rationalizations are ultimately self-defeating.

***"It's only a job. I'll put my real energy into my personal life."***
In her book, *Do What You Love, the Money Will Follow,* Marsha Sinetar explores the concept of "right livelihood":

*Right Livelihood is an idea about work which is linked to the natural order of things. It is doing our best at what we do best. The rewards are inevitable and manifold. There is no way we can fail. . . . Any talent we are born with eventually surfaces as a need. . . . The original concept of Right Livelihood apparently comes from the teachings of Buddha, who described it as work consciously chosen, done with full awareness and care, and leading to enlightenment . . .*

*Right Livelihood, in both its ancient and contemporary sense, embodies self-expression, commitment, mindfulness, and conscious choice. Finding and doing work of this sort is predicated upon high self-esteem, since only those who like themselves, who subjectively feel they are trustworthy and deserving, are able to choose on behalf of what is right and true for them. . . . When we consciously choose to do work we enjoy, not only can we get things done, we can get them done well and be intrinsically rewarded for the effort. Money and security cease to be our only payments.[1]*

It isn't easy to find and attain right livelihood. At a number of points in my own professional life, when I was unhappy with where I was but not yet ready to take action, I have either sought to detach myself emotionally from my work or longed for a position that was "just a job." For those who are passionate about their work—their right livelihood—but who are unable to financially support themselves in this work (the traditional starving artist comes to mind), it may be appropriate to seek out just a job. But for those of you who have not yet discovered your right livelihood, this approach will ensure that you never experience joy in work.

In my company, I like to say to software development teams who worry that they cannot meet a tight deadline, "Well, we may not make the deadline by trying. But I can guarantee that we *won't* meet it if we *don't* try." In the same vein, you may never find your right livelihood even if you diligently seek it, but how impoverished your life will be if you never begin the search!

Picasso called work "the ultimate seduction," and for people passionately engaged in any discipline, this description is undoubtedly true. They receive profound pleasure from working but always feel, regardless of their success, that they could do better. This tension between satisfaction and disappointment keeps them vital. The human spirit is like a muscle; without resistance and challenge, it not only fails to grow but atrophies.

*"It's too late for me to change careers."* One of our most distinguishing and poignant characteristics as humans is our awareness of our own mortality, or of the sense that it is too late for some things. But it is never too late to change. While the effects of time may reduce your ability to pursue certain goals, like being a professional athlete or a ballerina, there are always more opportunities than you have time to pursue. In my own life, whenever I've felt that it was too late to try something new, it was usually because I couldn't see a path between what I was then doing and a particular goal.

The word *path*, however, suggests that there is a fixed set of steps one must take to reach a goal, when in fact there is no such thing. The world is a place of uncertainty and accident, of opportunity and disaster. As a result, no one can chart a specific path to a specific future, but as with any journey in uncharted territory, you can choose a destination and route while expecting to encounter detours and roadblocks. In fact, if you can be open to these byways, you may have a much more exciting journey than you originally envisioned.

A wonderful painter once told me that the most common mistake amateur artists make is focusing too much on their original vision for a painting rather than remaining sensitive to what is happening on the canvas. The genius knows how to incorporate happy accidents into an ultimately more exciting result.

For apprentices who believe that they cannot succeed in their current job and who refuse to adopt either of the self-defeating attitudes described above, there are two choices—change jobs and look for a more fulfilling environment or graduate from apprentice to warrior.

Adopting a different attitude toward risk marks the apprentice's graduation. The ambitious apprentice longs to be judged worthy by his supervisors. He might be willing to accept assignments that could lead to failure but not to directly confront or attack his manager, even if he believes the manager is wrong. Thus, the apprentice is happy to let the manager define the playing field. Warriors, on the other hand, are convinced that they know what is right and are willing to risk failure and disapproval from both their managers and their peers to pursue what they consider victory. In short, apprentices tend to risk only with permission, while warriors are committed to any risk required to achieve what they believe is right.

If facing risk with commitment is a critical characteristic of personal and professional development, then the path to success is more like a battle plan. One commits to a battle plan only when one has committed to the war or to winning a battle in pursuit of some worthwhile end. But not even the greatest general can map out each action in a battle ahead of time. A battle plan is a strategy that, if the assumptions underlying that strategy prove false, may be quickly modified in favor of more opportunistic tactics. Moreover, as in war, personal development entails multiple battles, some of which will end in defeat. Your steadfast commitment to multiple engagements is critical to your success.

## Preparing for the Role of Warrior

If someone is truly dedicated to a goal, he or she expects to persevere in spite of failure. Consequently, it is rarely any single event that triggers the apprentice's decision to become a warrior.

The first time an apprentice's true contribution (or his perception of his true contribution) to an effort goes unappreciated, he is likely to assume that there was some innocent oversight or misunderstanding on the manager's part. But when this treatment occurs repeatedly, the ensuing frustration causes the apprentice either to hide in one of the ways described above or to assume the role of the warrior. Thus, professional growth often begins in hurt and disappointment.

Of course, it is possible that some failure on his own part, such as a flippant attitude or an inability to communicate, is blocking the apprentice's success. However, too often the apprentice's view of himself is inaccurate, cloudy, or more a reflection of what others see in him rather than what he is willing to discover about himself. As a result, even when most frustrated, he will tend to focus on external battles rather than seeking out inner enemies. In any case, the transition from apprentice to warrior usually occurs when chronic frustration gives way to anger, and the apprentice decides to force others to acknowledge his true value.

## Stage Two: The Warrior

The primary difference, then, between the apprentice and the warrior is that the warrior's goals sufficiently compel her to risk disapproval and engage in conflict, while the apprentice is not yet either dissatisfied or secure enough to assume such risk. With risk comes fear. So one of the most important tasks facing the new warrior is dealing with her own fear.

However, in my case at least, the emotion that I was most aware of in my early days of warfare was anger. My anger gave me the courage to speak out (too forcefully, I now recognize) to bosses whom I thought were wrong. Yet I didn't enjoy feeling or expressing anger. Few people do. In fact, frequently what I was angriest about was the very fact that the person I was in conflict with, or the enemy, had made me so mad.

What I have learned since then is that anger is the mask of fear, and fear is the mask of pain. Whenever I feel really angry, it's usually because at some level I feel threatened, and what I fear is that I will be hurt. When I've failed to look past my anger to understand my fear, I've wound up making more enemies and fighting more battles than necessary.

The warrior is committed to victory over the enemy, which in business is the person, people, or organization preventing the warrior's success. The warrior's goal may be personal achievement—for example, a promotion to vice president—or some form of success for the organization in terms of product or profits. In either case, to achieve that goal, the warrior must be willing to risk failure and disgrace. In so doing, she must learn to hold her fear in check while performing at the peak of her skills. As a result, playing the role of warrior can lead to significant spiritual growth. The bulk of this book will focus on techniques, both good and bad, for skillfully conducting warfare in the workplace.

## Common Misconceptions by the Warrior
Just as apprentices frequently adopt attitudes that constrain their progress, warriors often exhibit certain attitudes that can be equally limiting.

*"I have to prove him wrong."* The warrior's role is to fight for what she believes is right. Thus, the warrior has much invested in seeing her values and opinions acknowledged. To avoid or back down from a battle is a sign of cowardice. Consequently, the warrior will sometimes take on enemies without regard for the pain and effort required to combat them.

I was aware that both of my first two bosses in the business world took an instant dislike to me when they interviewed me. In fact, the second one actually said to me, "Well, J. H. is a big gorilla around here, so if he wants to hire you, I guess we're going to hire you." The comment made it abundantly clear that I was not *his* choice. If I'd had a more positive focus on what I wanted to achieve at that point in my career, I probably would have turned down both positions or at least requested to work for someone else. However, I was convinced that since my motives were pure—I only wanted what was best for the company—these men didn't have the right to prejudge me, and I would simply have to prove them wrong. It was the Daddy thing surfacing again. I subsequently had to learn an important lesson about proving people wrong: *If you think it would require therapy to fix your boss, leave.*

Sure enough, in both positions I spent half my energy trying to get these men to acknowledge that I was right. In the first position, I kept thinking that my boss had simply misjudged me because he didn't understand my arguments, and I became more and more agitated and angry as all my efforts to convince him failed. I prevailed against this boss only by circumventing his authority and convincing *his* boss that I was right.

Perhaps it was my winning this first battle that made me confront my second boss more quickly. But, as I will discuss later, I didn't win the latter battle, and my career took a nosedive. In fact, I sustained such a powerful emotional loss that it made me rethink my need to be right.

*"Everyone must understand."* Because having their own sense of justice vindicated is critical to warriors, they will often try to enlist others' support by taking their case to the people in search of allies. Of course, this search differs from those who never graduate to warrior, drop out of career growth, and spend their time bitching to others in the coffee room about perceived injustices, which they use as excuses for not taking action or as signs that "nothing can be done." Even warriors who know that they will undertake the battle alone will fre-

quently seek support from others for their cause, but simply because it is so important to them *that they be proved right*.

Trying to win supporters, however, especially when it involves assassinating the enemy's character, frequently backfires. Then the warrior looks like someone with an ax to grind rather than a proponent of what is just.

My own experience in fighting my second boss is a perfect example about how seeking sympathy can backfire. I found this individual's attitude toward women intolerable. He regularly belittled his wife to others (mocking her driving and her mistakes); he remarked that he wasn't sure that he approved of a pregnant colleague's plan to come back to work after her baby arrived; and he consistently sent me signals that he thought my opinions were "out of line." But because I showed anger when I complained about his behavior to my (mostly male) colleagues, I came off as a strident, over-the-top feminist and actually garnered him sympathy.

**"He [or she] is a horrible human being."** While apprentices are characterized by their need for judgment, warriors are characterized by their need to judge. Thus, the warrior's rage is often disproportional to the severity of the shortcomings or "sins" of the enemy. In this way, the warrior can convince himself that battle is inevitable and that the consequences of not fighting would be unthinkable.

### Outgrowing the Role of Warrior
While learning to be an effective warrior requires significant personal growth, the warrior's role can also become frustrating. In the real world, bad ideas and opinions abound. If one's goal is to defeat these enemies, there will always be another enemy to defeat. Rather than focusing on the positive aspects of work such as creation, profit, and success, the warrior is always focused on the negatives: understanding the opponent's weaknesses, taking pleasure in his mistakes, and being

enraged by his ruthlessness, stupidity, or lack of ethics. Furthermore, whenever one engages in battle, one always assumes the risk of defeat, and defeat can sometimes be devastating.

In my own case, an impressive defeat at the hands of my second boss made me rethink the desirability of living the warrior's life. As I indicated above, I made no secret of the things and people I liked and (especially) disliked during that period. As a result, when I was working in the computer-aided design (CAD) program at MCC,[2] I won the reputation of being a sharp-tongued, difficult person and so was not as capable of garnering allies as I should have been. My boss supported a "secret" research project aimed at replacing the work T and I had been doing. We had wind of it, but there was nothing we could do except keep our heads down, focus on our work, and wait to see the secret project publicly unveiled.

On the appointed day, I was approached at lunch and told to come to a meeting in the afternoon and *not* to bring T. When I arrived, the entire research staff was present, and the team in charge of the new work was given the floor to present the new approach followed by several researchers from other labs who indicated that they preferred the new approach. After about an hour and a half of this, the vice president of the program turned to me and asked, "Do you have anything to say?"

Well, I may be bullheaded, but I'm not stupid. I can recognize a massacre when I see one. Dismayed by the solidarity of so many people intent on my defeat, I replied, "I don't think there is anything to say. It seems that you have made up your minds."

After the meeting, my boss, hardly able to contain his glee, said to me, "Kay, that was the most professional I've ever seen you behave."

Later, the manager of another lab and another colleague told me that I had handled the meeting with dignity. I took the opportunity to ask, "Why on earth was it necessary to assemble the entire research staff for such a meeting rather than simply canceling our project?"

My colleague explained, "They were afraid of your reaction."

I said, "Well, if my reactions are *that* formidable, someone ought to contact the Department of Defense. I could become a new secret weapon."

I sounded tough, but I was really hurt. I had always gone to war believing that as long as I was fighting for the good of the company eventually I would prevail. I hadn't prepared myself, however, for what it felt like to have someone, or rather so many people, take pleasure in my defeat. In pondering this experience I became aware of the mistakes I had made in undertaking this war: showing my anger, becoming personally vituperative, and needing to be proved right. As a result, I determined that from then on it was less important to be judged right by other people than to be personally satisfied with what I was doing and where I was. I would risk what it took to achieve my goal—I would even go to war as a last resort—but I would never again make the same mistakes that had earned me so much enmity (or so I thought).

## Stage Three: The Adventurer

Every warrior will eventually experience a defeat that takes her out of the war. It may be the result of retirement, a layoff, sickness, or death, but no one wins forever. When a certain kind of defeat comes early enough or often enough, however, it may cause the warrior to reexamine her values and make the transition to adventurer. The motivation for making this transition is not always negative. In a few rare cases, someone acquires the skills of a warrior so easily that her early conquests lead her to discount the enemy and thereby the value of battle, and she finds that she prefers instead to focus on other activities.

While apprentices focus on approval and warriors on vindication, adventurers focus on challenge and discovery. They value respect, friendship, and recognition, but they do not need these things. They recognize that evil exists and accept that it will always exist, and while they are not afraid of war, they do not have the warrior's need to conquer evil or to be proved right. The warrior feels that he must defeat any evil he encounters and spends most of his energy preparing for or engaged in warfare. The adventurer recognizes evil but will fight it only when battle is unavoidable, favoring instead finding a path around, under, or through the evil.[3] Part of what enables the adventurer to take this approach is that he values his own judgment over that of anyone else. As a result, the adventurer is free to let others hold whatever opinions they choose.

I was more or less forced into adopting the life of the adventurer after the research project was canceled. T and I had been right in what we fought for—the new program that superseded ours eventually failed, and the behavior of my boss and his cronies helped precipitate that failure—but our being right didn't matter. Our research project had been canceled, and for the first time in my life I was perceived as a problem and a troublemaker.

I suppose I could have sucked it in, hidden my feelings, and tried to work my way back into the good graces of the other people in the program. However, that would have been hypocritical, because, you see, I still thought I was right. Instead I realized that other people don't necessarily see the world the way you do. They can get just as frustrated when someone else tries to force another viewpoint, particularly if that person is judgmental, angry, or personal when doing so.

I decided that as long as I could pursue a professional path where I believed in what I was doing and could minimize the need for support from others, it didn't matter what people thought of me or my opinions. But my colleague T and I were miserable at MCC. We talked about starting a gag gift company. (We had a rather dark sense of humor at the time. Most of our gift ideas were of a male-bashing and somewhat bawdy variety.) We also toyed with the idea of starting a software company. We had a good idea—to build a retargetable code generator that could serve as a long-term solution for allowing companies to automate the task of writing interfaces to keep related data consistent, regardless of where it resided—but neither of us had the spare time to start a new venture. T had a number of personal interests that claimed her hours outside of work, and I had an ailing father and two teenage daughters, one of whom was giving me fits. Realizing that neither of us had the drive or energy outside the workday to be effective in a new undertaking, I was faced with the prospect of finding another programming job. I couldn't stand that thought.

In fact, my dread at having to find another programming job led me to embark on my path as an adventurer. I could have found another job at the same or better pay, but I couldn't stand the job itself—having to commit arbitrarily to another team and to another do-or-die schedule—and the way organizations in large companies invariably work at cross-purposes to the detriment of the whole. I could no longer, as a mercenary, fight someone else's war. What was more important to me was working on something I believed in.

So I took the idea that T and I had for a software product, wrote a proposal for a research project to investigate this area, and shopped it around MCC to see if we could get funding to pursue it. To do this legwork I had to swallow my pride, because most people at MCC at that point—after my excesses as a warrior in the CAD program—thought of me as irrational and difficult. But my strategy was to focus on the goal—getting funding for the project. (And privately I thought, If T and I could get this done, we should start a company.)

I didn't know what each step would entail and had no idea whether I could succeed. In fact, I thought I would probably fail. I then decided that what I needed to focus on was not whether I would ultimately succeed or fail, but the next step—

what I could do, given the circumstances, to move forward. Note that I was not caught up in issues of fairness or justice but in tackling the next set of things that could be done.

The rest is history. We obtained funding for the research project, and in January 1991, Robin Curle and I left MCC (T had moved on to another career opportunity) with six other people to found Evolutionary Technologies, which until the late 90s was one of the fastest-growing companies in the United States. Since that time, I have had more personal success and recognition than I ever dreamed possible, and I've fought my share of battles in the process. While I still value all the skills I learned in becoming a warrior, I no longer take pleasure either in battle itself or in the enemy's defeat. Nevertheless, I am convinced that the key to my professional growth and personal satisfaction lay in acquiring the skills of the warrior and understanding the nature of war.

## Work as Warfare

Before we consider the kinds of battles we face as workplace warriors, I want to take a moment to discuss the appropriateness of using a war metaphor for the struggles we face in the workplace. Because I am a woman (well, some days I feel like a woman), some might attribute this choice of metaphor to strident feminism, but that is not the case. *Esquire* magazine once ran a cover and feature story entitled "Why Men Love War." The gist of the article was that it is in situations where life itself is at risk that the chaff of our day-to-day existence is recognized for what it is. In war, individuals are forced to draw on the deepest reserves of their heart and spirit. It is perhaps for this reason that so many religions focus on the "battle" between good and evil. War is the archetype of any all-engrossing struggle between right and wrong, and it is natural to think of workplace conflicts as a form of warfare.

However, the metaphor is even more apt when one

considers the greater risks we experience today as a result of the increased rate of social and technological change. More than twenty years ago, in his book *Future Shock*, Alvin Toffler wrote that five relationships, plus time, constitute social experience:

> *This is why . . . things, places, people, organizations, and ideas are the basic components of all situations. It is the individual's distinctive relationship to each of these components that structures the situation.*
>
> *And it is precisely these relationships that, as acceleration occurs in society, become foreshortened, telescoped in time. Relationships that once endured for long spans of time now have shorter life expectancies. It is this abbreviation, this compression that gives rise to the most tangible feeling that we live, rootless and uncertain, among shifting dunes.*[4]

Toffler argued that, with continued accelerated change, the individuals who could live most comfortably in the future would be those who could rapidly abandon one set of assumptions and adopt another. Few of us today would disagree with his insights, particularly with respect to the business world. Since 1985 we have seen the death or absorption of many large and successful companies, such as International Harvester and General Dynamics. With these changes has come the displacement of thousands of white- and blue-collar workers. Moreover, the increased centralization and globalization of production, whether industrial or agricultural, raises the likelihood of even greater volatility.

These large-scale changes in operations impact entire communities. In one particularly poignant example, in May 1989, Control Data Corporation closed ETA, its supercomputer subsidiary, and laid off 3,300 people in the Minneapolis-St. Paul area. What is striking about this particular plant closing was the way it was handled. ETA employees arrived at work on a Monday morning to find the doors locked and buses waiting in the parking lot. They were taken to a nearby auditorium—ironically, the same one that served to house Garrison Keillor's radio show, *A Prairie Home Companion,* with its gently humorous, nostalgic view of life in a traditional, close-knit middle-American community. However, on that day, the members of the audience were told that they no longer had jobs and would have thirty minutes in the presence of a guard to gather their belongings at the plant.

Consider their situation:

If you were one of 3,300 people laid off in a single day in the Minneapolis–St. Paul area, could you sell your house? (Could anybody in the community sell their house without losing a significant amount of equity?)

Were you likely to find another comparable job without moving?

What had happened to your odds of sending your children to college or of enjoying a comfortable retirement?

How were your recovery prospects affected by the fact that during the same week Kodak laid off 4,500 people and DEC announced a plan to lay off 7,000 workers over a two-year period?

The solution is not to blame management or the heartlessness of big business. As I've learned, managing a business has its own set of problems and heartaches. In some situations, downsizing is arguably necessary for the company's survival. The important point to recognize is that, in many cases, the company neither can nor will give workers advance notice. (Under the circumstances, an early retirement program can be considered a philanthropic gesture.) Consequently, unless you want to run the risk of being taken by surprise, it's up to you to track the economic forces at work in your industry or the industries upon which you depend. Be proactive in guarding your own well-being. No one else will do it for you.

As we move into the twenty-first century, the economic forces at play with the globalization of the economy and the increasingly rapid rate of change constitute an exciting but volatile backdrop for personal development. The gap between the haves and the have-nots is widening, and no one can assume that her affiliation with a particular group can protect her from harm. In short, more and more reasons abound for individuals to acquire the skills of a workplace warrior.

## Notes

1. Marsha Sinetar, *Do What You Love, the Money Will Follow* (Mahwah, N.J.: Paulist Press, 1987), pp. 8–10.

2. The official name of MCC is Microelectronics and Computer Technology Corporation. Founded in 1983, it was the first industry-backed, for-profit, computer research consortium in the United States.

3. I first heard this distinction between the warrior and the adventurer in a workshop held by Serge King, author and proponent of Huna, the traditional shamanism of Hawaii.

4. Alvin Toffler, *Future Shock* (New York: Bantam, 1971), pp. 45–46.

# section I

# Rules of Engagement

# Chapter 1

# The Regional Conflict
## Issues in Running a Private Company*

**W**e are a culture of strong opinions. Our need to judge others and make pronouncements may come from some aspect of the human soul, but the U.S. tradition of free speech coupled with the immediacy of the media and its passion for opinion have led to two unfortunate national traits—a tendency to oversimplify and a cynicism that is too often used to rationalize the failure to take personal responsibility. We encounter examples of people passing blame every day. An elderly woman who spills coffee and burns herself when leaving McDonald's sues because the coffee was too hot. The family of a man who smoked for twenty years and died of lung cancer sues the tobacco company for more than he would have earned if he had lived another forty years. We want lower taxes but are dismayed when defense spending is cut and jobs are lost. If our net worth is affected when a company doesn't make its expected earnings, management must have been incompetent or corrupt.

Our national preoccupation with blame and judgment and what's unfair may be therapeutic to many and profitable to

*As pointed out in the Preface, the material in chapters 1 and 2 is particularly geared to entrepreneurs.

some, but it won't change the fact that forces are at work in the global economy that we cannot control through legislation. In fact, survival in business often requires that a company find a way around these forces or constraints that limit its ability to grow, because with rare exceptions, if a company can't grow, it dies. Just as animals may compete for the same resources in a geographic region, companies and countries compete in the marketplace, and the results can be devastating to the less powerful. While modern business practices focus on "win-win" negotiations, rarely does one venture's success not adversely affect the status of another. In short, most businesses are at war. And in any war there are winners and losers. No amount of rationalizing or finger-pointing can change that.

These two chapters focus on characterizing the rules of war for two types of companies—private companies with external investors and public companies. You can have a successful professional life without understanding this information, just as you can be a successful soldier without knowing how to wage war. Mercenaries sell their skills while loyal soldiers demonstrate courage in battle after battle, many without understanding the larger plan behind each engagement. For any hope of victory, however, management must have a larger plan, and one hard truth every leader in warfare knows is that sacrificing certain troops for the well-being of others is sometimes necessary. As a result, particularly in today's rapidly evolving business climate, even if you choose to be a soldier rather than a general, you should understand the war you are fighting and how it is being waged. After all, your livelihood may someday be sacrificed for some greater economic good.

If you are knowledgeable about economics and business, some of the following may be obvious, and you might decide to skip this chapter. But if you do not handle your own investments and are not knowledgeable about how private and public companies are governed, like I was for most of my life, this material is probably worth reading. For the first forty years of my life, I had no appreciation for how business worked from an economic point of view. Like a soldier who is solely focused on the enemy coming over the ridge, my sights were focused on complaining that the raises the university gave to the faculty didn't even match the inflation rate or on wondering how Texas Instruments, a hardware manufacturer, expected my team to meet an aggressive programming deadline when we only had three workstations for six programmers. I could really work myself into a lather about the shortsightedness of management. What's more is that I was right. What I didn't see, however, was that my battle was only one of thousands being waged within the organizations, most of which were more important than my own.

My later experiences in founding and running a private company and what I have learned about running a public company have led me to appreciate the potential for conflict between management, shareholders, and employees: the motivations of each class of players, their fears about each other, the situations where conflict is inherent due to the very terms of the relationship, and some views about the best compromise that management can hope for. I hope this information will help you better assess what kind of war the company you are working for is waging, how to perform more effectively in your particular battles, and how to recognize when your prospect of victory seems slim.

## The Mind of the General

People start companies for a variety of reasons. Probably the worst reason for starting a company is to get rich and retire. There is nothing wrong about wanting financial independence, but to be successful a business must bring value. Any entrepreneur who focuses primarily on what a business can give him is probably not paying enough attention to what his company should be doing for the customer.

Some of the most successful companies were started by people who were convinced that their previous employers were seriously flawed in some way. Consider the case of TI and the personal computer (PC). TI decided to build its first personal computer to be incompatible with the IBM PC, reasoning that IBM's consumer base would abandon the IBM hardware and the thousands of associated software packages available because TI's keyboard was more ergonomic and its graphics superior. After violently arguing with management that this reasoning made no sense, Rod Canion and two engineers from TI founded Compaq Computer. Eighteen years and an expensive lawsuit later, Compaq became the second largest computer company in the world, while TI no longer manufactured or sold computers.

Regardless of the reason for founding a company, every entrepreneur faces the question of what is the best way to fund initial operations. If the entrepreneur is sufficiently well-off, he or she might initially fund the company out of private assets. However, this approach is questionable for a number of reasons. First, if the idea for a product or service is sufficiently strong and the chief executive officer (CEO) of the start-up sells it effectively, then it should be possible to raise money. Second, even if the product or service is good, the market strong, and the management team effective, the odds are that the company will not be as successful as hoped. Consequently, if an individual has risked a retirement fund or a home, there is a good chance that he or she will lose that investment at the end of the venture.

Raising money from friends and family may seem like the next easiest way to raise capital, but it almost always causes headaches. Few companies reach their most optimistic goals, and successful companies frequently require significantly more time and capital than originally envisioned. Unless the friends and family are led by a business angel in whom they have faith and who is not surprised by the inevitable delays and disappointments, the friends and family are likely to become disenchanted, talk among themselves, and require significant energy on the entrepreneur's part to manage. Also, dealing with the guilt when Aunt Hattie needs access to her funds is simply an aggravation that someone trying to build a business doesn't need.

As a result, unless a company can be bootstrapped—that is, grown with little or no capital investment—the first-time entrepreneur at some point will seek capital from professional investors. Understanding their concerns and how they grade prospective investments can help in developing the business plan and the basic pitch for investment partners. Equally important is understanding the kind of risks one encounters when taking on this kind of investor.

## The First Battle: Finding Investors

Running a household and running a business have a surprising amount in common: the need for sound fiscal management, the delegation of authority, and the obligation to provide for the benefit of the group's members. In the case of small family- or privately owned companies, even if friends and families have in part funded them, the analogy holds. Whether these companies grow at 10 percent or 50 percent a year is a function of what the owners want and what the competition will tolerate in terms of scale or service. As long as these companies provide products customers want—whether it's pet sitting or premium wines—the small private company can survive, unless some significantly larger organization, such as Walmart, offers sufficient price benefits to offset other less tangible benefits like convenience or personal attention.

In any case, just like families, all companies at one point or another need access to more money than they have in order to fund growth. However, while the family and the established company both have access to capital through banks, the small private company usually has to seek funds from investors who specialize in high-risk investments. These professional investors, whether business "angels" or venture capitalists, invest in private companies because they expect them to grow at a sufficiently high rate to yield a return superior to what they could earn in other, less risky investments. Moreover, unless these investors expect the company to buy them out at some minimum predetermined rate at a particular time (in which case the investment is more of a loan), they expect a "liquidity" event—either the sale of the company or a public offering—so they can realize their profits and have the opportunity to move on.

While you personally may never have to be involved with raising money, you can be certain that there is a person or people who work at your company for whom this is one of their primary concerns. Just as it is important for individuals to maintain good credit and adequate resources to survive some interruption to their income, companies must have sufficient cash on hand to fund operations or to look like a sound enough financial entity to be able to raise or borrow money. The remainder of Section I focuses on the challenge faced by the management of small private companies in raising cash, the repercussions of following one strategy versus another, and the effects these choices may have on the company's employees.

It's relatively easy to interest investors in a going concern that has a strong record for growth in profits. It's much harder to raise money to start a company. Occasionally, a no-brainer, a product like Viagra, has such obvious appeal that it is clearly a winner, but in most cases, neither the entrepreneur nor the story is that compelling. As a result, too often the relationship forged between the investors and management is like an uneasy alliance between ethnic groups that have experienced centuries of distrust. Any crack in the structure causes chaos. However, for entrepreneurs who cannot bootstrap their companies and who (in most cases, wisely) choose not to use funds from friends and family, there are two primary sources of professional capital—business angels and venture capitalists.

## What Drives the Business Angel

Business angels are wealthy individuals, often self-made or with considerable business background, who allocate some of their resources to invest seed money in new ventures. The advantage of a business angel is that the only person's money at risk is his own. In other words, the business angel has no one to answer to if the company fails. As a result, first-time entrepreneurs just starting a company often find it easier to raise money from angels than from traditional venture capital firms, and depending upon the individual in question, the relationship may be either hands-off or very involved.

Business angels rarely consider themselves to be the company's last investor. Their goal is to provide the entrepreneur with enough capital to fund initial product development and sales so that the company can later raise additional capital at a higher valuation than at which they invested. The careful business angel, however, will take pains to ensure that the company is run soundly, or he runs the risk that the company will be unable to raise that additional capital.

## What Drives the Venture Capitalist

While some business angels consider their investments almost a hobby, venture capitalists are in the business of making and managing high-risk investments on behalf of their limited partners, which can range from wealthy individuals to pension funds. Investors in venture funds understand that the investments made by venture capitalists (VCs) run a higher risk of failing than other more conservative investments, because VC-funded companies rarely have significant assets or revenue history. These investors take this risk because they expect the venture capitalists to be savvy about the marketplace and responsible for the management of the companies in which they invest, and while individual investments may lose money, the overall performance of the sum total of investments will provide good returns.

Each VC fund raised has a limited duration, at the end of which the venture capitalists must cash out. If venture capitalists do not provide an above-average return on the sum of the investments, they may not be able to raise their next round of funding. As a result, one of the VC's most important tasks is evaluating a company prior to investment, because once the check has been written, there's no backing out. The term frequently applied to this type of evaluation in the business arena is *due diligence* and refers to the steps that one party takes to ensure that the representations made by another party are accurate. In the case of evaluating start-up companies, this process involves assessing a number of relatively complex issues discussed below.

**The Product.** If the product has not yet been produced, the merits of the proposed products and the likelihood that the company's team has sufficient skill and experience to produce the product must be evaluated. If the product exists, the VC will want to obtain customer references.

**Its Potential Market.** Because VCs want a high rate of return, two of their biggest concerns are the size of the market for the company's proposed products or services and the company's potential to succeed in capturing a large share of that market. There is considerable art involved in evaluating the potential merits of and markets for a product. As a result, many venture firms specialize and hire associates based on their expertise and experience in a particular area. However, even when VCs have considerable expertise in particular areas, it is often hard for them to assess the potential of a proposal—in part because the entrepreneurs do such a bad job of articulating why the product is important from a business standpoint. For example, I recall counseling a couple who had not been able to raise money for what they had benchmarks to prove was the best data compression technology available anywhere. They dropped their jaws in unison when I asked why their idea was important and exactly who was spending too much because this technology was not available. To them the answer was obvious—anyone sending data from one place to another (in short, anyone using the Internet). To the VCs, it was technical jargon.

**The Current Ownership of the Company.** In order to have a legal entity with which the VC can interact, the entrepreneurs must establish some kind of corporation and, in so doing, determine which founders own how much of the company's stock. The cleaner the ownership, the better from the VC's point of view. If the company has funded its initial operations out of the entrepreneurs' savings or an investment from a business angel, the VC is frequently comforted, as this shows the founders' level of commitment and sophistication. If, however, the initial funds have been raised from friends and family, it can pose problems when structuring a deal where decisions need to be made quickly and efficiently. For this reason, VCs are frequently attracted to companies that have already raised funds from other reputable VCs, because they can assume that these issues have already been resolved.

**The Financial Status of the Company.** Determining this status entails understanding the amount of cash on hand and the way that cash is managed and accounted for. In a start-up, the entrepreneur frequently keeps the company's books as if it's a household, with bills and receipts in a shoebox, checks written by hand, and so on. Others are more sophisticated and use a service for payroll, and still others keep a proper set of financials. In any case, VCs need to assure themselves that the company's management is fiscally responsible, for example, with respect to payroll taxes and sales taxes. If a company fails to manage its finances properly, the entrepreneur will find it extremely hard to raise money even if the shortcoming is addressed, because the VC will worry about what other oversights might have occurred.

***Intellectual Property and Dependence on Key Personnel.*** If the product development is dependent upon proprietary technology, the VC must verify that the company has protected its intellectual property through patents, license, copyright, or the appropriate treatment of trade secret material. When the utilization or further development of this technology is dependent upon the know-how and skills of one or two people, the VC needs assurance regarding the company's ability to retain those key persons or plan for recovery if that is not possible.

***The Management.*** Finally, and probably most important, the VC is concerned with the management team. Building a successful company takes more than simply having a better mousetrap. As one vice president (VP) of sales and marketing says, "If the best product always won, there would be one kind of everything." Being successful in business requires appreciation for the potential pitfalls and complexity of managing expenditures, people, development, customer support, and so forth. Moreover, the processes required to manage these areas effectively change as a company grows. Given that VCs are satisfied with their other areas of due diligence, their biggest risk then is that the people running the company do not have the experience, skills, or character to run the company. With the first-time entrepreneur VCs have even more concern. Reference checks in these cases can uncover a great deal about the entrepreneur's character or particular set of skills, for example, technical or marketing. However, the fact remains that someone who has never run a company poses a bigger risk than someone who has. In my case, for example, I was considered a poor risk for a CEO. I had neither experience nor training in business, and my background was technical. Even worse, my partner and I were both women in our forties in 1991, long before being a woman CEO was fashionable.

At any rate, the skills of the management team are one of the most important factors leading to a company's success and one of the hardest for a potential investor to measure. Even if one or more of the investors is local and can regularly visit the company, the company's success will depend on the ability of management to assess the company's progress on a daily basis. To offset this risk, many VCs insist on augmenting the management team as a condition of investing.

## Achieving Détente after the Funding

There are two mind-sets with which an entrepreneur can approach raising money—one that assumes success and a benign world and one that is characterized by a degree of cynicism. Dark, Polish soul that I am, I tended toward the latter, in part because I was aware of how little I knew and I was afraid that if I were too open and trusting, my naïveté would not serve me well in the funding process. But whether the entrepreneur is optimistic or cynical, the terms and conditions of the early rounds of funding determine who has how much to say about how the company is run, and that can seriously affect the fate of the company and the future of all employees. All companies stumble at one point or another. If it is a private company, the decision regarding how to proceed in large part is determined by who has control, and that is a function of the terms and conditions of its funding.

### Determining How Much Money to Raise

Two groups control a company—the board and the shareholders. The board's charter is to ensure that the company is run ethically and in the best interests of the shareholders. Decisions regarding ownership—such as whether to go public, sell, or declare bankruptcy—are determined by the majority of the shareholders and whether any group within the shareholders has veto power. (Such powers are often required by minority investors on later rounds of investment.)

In a private company, the board usually consists of representatives of the investors and the company's management. The board's size and makeup can seriously affect management's freedom in running the company. On the initial round of funding, most VCs like having a "second"—that is, at least one other venture capitalist who participates in the deal—to share the risk in case the company needs additional capital before it shows substantive progress. In this way, no single firm stands to lose too much on a deal that doesn't go as expected.

If the entrepreneur takes money from more than one VC on the initial round, however, it is likely that each will want a board seat. This condition has two disadvantages. First, unless the company is able to have as many board seats as investors, the entrepreneur has just unfavorably shifted the balance of power in governing the company. Since investors on any subsequent round usually also require board representation, the number of votes accorded the company's management decreases over time. Therefore, taking money from a number of VCs on the initial round can accelerate the time at which the company loses control of the board.

VCs also tend to encourage management to raise more money than the company thinks it needs on the initial round to ensure that the company will not need to seek additional capital before it has sufficient sales history to argue for a higher valuation (that is, what the new investors think the company is worth). While this approach is prudent, it also increases the likelihood that the company will lose control on the initial round of funding.

The trade-off management faces in any funding event is the amount of money being raised versus the price the investor is paying. The goal is to raise enough money to advance the company's financial performance sufficiently to ensure that the next stock offering is sold at a higher price. In fact, the company's skill in making these trade-off decisions and in successfully executing within the parameters of those decisions is exactly what drives the economy and causes the drama we see in the stock market. But the trade-offs made in the first round of funding can affect whether the company survives to raise another round. Therefore, it is critical that management achieve an effective détente in this first round.

## Understanding the VC's Fear

Investing in a start-up company run by a first-time entrepreneur is something akin to a mail-order marriage. The pictures and letters might have been convincing, but immediately after the ceremony a sense of uncertainty sets in. While much of the due diligence performed in the process of making a later-stage investment is based on a considerable amount of sales history, the VC investing in a start-up is investing in a dream. For this reason, VCs frequently demand that one of the investors be local or that they bring in a senior manager. While neither of these actions is particularly damning, it is important to remember the fear that drives them, to assume that the VCs are skeptical, and to behave accordingly. Otherwise, if the entrepreneur is too open and too obviously green, he or she may lead VC investors to believe that they need even more protection.

For the first-time entrepreneur, having a VC recommend an experienced manager is potentially dangerous because that manager's opinions may carry more weight with the VC than those of any of the founders. Likewise, any naïveté on the entrepreneur's part is sure to be reported, thereby further undermining the VC's faith in the founder's management skills. Almost no venture proceeds without one or more crises, and one of the worst things that can happen in such situations is when the management team dwells on who is right or appears the most knowledgeable rather than focusing on how the problem can be solved. If the entrepreneur becomes emotional in dealing with such conflicts, it becomes extremely easy for the VC to argue for even more changes in management.

## Conflicts Inherent in the Relationship

It is important to understand the conflicts inherent in a relationship in order to manage it. VCs are primarily responsible to only one class of individual, that is, the limited partners who invested in their fund(s). The entrepreneur is responsible to three parties: the customers for the product or services, the investors, and the employees, who, of course, include themselves. Even when things are going well, at least two situations involving the entrepreneur's commitment to the employees or customers may lead to a conflict with the VC investor—valuation of private rounds and agreeing on an exit strategy, discussed later.

*Valuation of Private Rounds.* The legal terms under which most VC investment are made include the right to buy enough shares on subsequent rounds to maintain their initial percentage of ownership on subsequent private rounds. As a result, the VC investors may agree that the company needs to raise an additional round and agree to the amount of the round, but they may not want the same level of valuation as the company since the greater the valuation the more they will have to pay for their additional shares. Meanwhile, the company, particularly the management and those employees who have a significant number of shares, will want to minimize the number of shares issued to obtain the capital so as to negligibly dilute their position.

VCs will argue, and justifiably so, that the value of an employee's stock should be determined by the company's success and not by what percentage of the company any particular employee owns. However, there are at least two cases where the number of shares issued can adversely affect management's interest. In situations where a vote determines whether the company pursues a particular course—for example, being acquired—if management and the employees no longer have a controlling percentage, then their wishes may be overridden. In the second case, if too many shares are issued before the company pursues liquidity, then it may be necessary at some point to perform a reverse split, where employees receive fewer numbers of shares than they previously owned as part of the transaction. Reverse splits don't affect how much an employee's stock is worth. Three hundred shares valued at $10.00 a share is worth the same as 3,000 shares valued at $1.00 a share, but if the employee has been "counting his chickens," a reverse split can be demoralizing. (Nevertheless, many success stories include a reverse split before an initial public offering [IPO]. For example, Tivoli Systems executed a reverse 3-for-1 split before their IPO in 1995, which was a wild success and was followed in March, 1996 by a $743 million cash purchase by IBM.)

## How Control of the Boardroom Affects the Soldier's Life

If you choose to be a soldier rather than a general, incentive stock option plans—and the value of that stock over time—can greatly affect your financial security. This possibility is no great surprise now that we are used to reading about the "Microsoft millionaires" or stories of ordinary employees who were in the right place at the right time. However, for every success there are many failures. When we started ETI, the popular wisdom was that one out of every ten companies funded by VCs perform wildly above expectations, three succeed in some capacity, and six fail and return less than invested. If you are among the growing numbers of people who take a job with a start-up with the hope of retiring rich, it behooves you to be aware of these statistics. You should also understand your company's funding strategy and assess whether it is working in terms of ultimately giving you a return, that is, a way to turn the stock you have into cash or a publicly traded security.

***Agreeing on the Exit Strategy.*** Control of the company is often an important factor in how early investors and employees achieve liquidity. The VCs' need for an exit strategy within a fixed period may make them want the company to pursue an acquisition or an IPO sooner than management would otherwise feel comfortable. When the stock market is performing adequately, VCs prefer a public offering because it tends to provide a better return. Once the company's stock is public, the VC can simply transfer the stock to the limited partners and count the return on his investment based on the price per share at the time of the transfer.

The situation isn't so clean for the entrepreneur or the early employees, however. Usually a six-month lockup period occurs after a company goes public during which neither the private investors nor the insiders—that is, the VCs, the entrepreneur and the employees—can sell their stock. Just as with private investors, when people invest in a public company, they want to believe that the company will continue to grow and that their investment will make money. One of the signs that investors and analysts use to gauge whether the company's prospects are good is the behavior of the entrepreneur or major inside stockholders. Presumably if insiders have faith that the company will continue to do well, they will hold onto their stock, knowing that it will ultimately be worth more. If insiders sell a large amount of stock, a panic can ensue and cause the stock's value to drop, which in these litigious times, can lead to a shareholder class action suit. As a result, entrepreneurs can't easily "cash their check" on a public offering. At most they can usually sell only 5 to 10 percent of their stock at the offering and are advised to sell limited amounts on a regular basis afterward.

The company's financial strength at the time of an initial public offering is therefore even more important to the employee than to the VC investor. If the company continues to show strong growth in earnings and profits for two to three years after the public offering, everyone wins. However, if it does not perform, the VC is hurt less than the entrepreneur or employees, because the VC's interest in the company can be distributed across a greater number of investors who have more freedom to trade the stock. The value of a public company's stock can decrease rapidly and remain depressed for a long period if the company fails to perform. Moreover, while even the largest companies can experience wild fluctuations in their stock value, it is hard for a new public company to recover from disappointing the market predominantly because it does not have a track record. Because their financial well-being is more closely tied to the continued success of the company, entrepreneurs and employees potentially have a great deal to lose if they believe that the company is going public prematurely, that is, before it is sufficiently positioned to perform consistently.

If the private investors become impatient for an exit and they have control, they can force the management of a company that is not performing as well as hoped into a merger or acquisition. Mergers and acquisitions are popular techniques for allowing companies to increase their revenue while decreasing their costs. However, even with the strongest companies, mergers and acquisitions are not without their disruptions for they require restructuring the management and frequently involve personnel cuts in the area where staff is duplicated.

Mergers and acquisitions can be even trickier for the management and early employees in a private company. If the private company is acquired by a public company with a strong record, the transaction can actually provide better liquidity. Even though there are some limitations on how quickly the entrepreneur or employee can sell his or her stock, the likelihood of the stock holding its value is often better than in the case of a new public company. However, if both companies are private or the acquiring company is not strong and is making the acquisition to bolster its position, the entrepreneur is likely to have less control and less assurance that the acquisition will lead to the positive outcome he was hoping for. Moreover, a merger and acquisition event can have even more effect on employees than on the principals or investors because one goal of such a transaction is to reduce expenses—in other words, head count—by leveraging off economy of scale. Thus, anyone serving as a soldier or lieutenant in a private company has even more to lose than a general.

## My Personal Experiences with VC Investors

Evolutionary Technologies International, Inc. (ETI) had a unique background in that, unlike most start-ups, we had the luxury of performing our basic research and development on somebody else's money at a research consortium. While this arrangement significantly reduced the amount of capital we needed to get our product to market, it offered a unique set of challenges when starting a company. I might have been discouraged from undertaking the task had I not been so inexperienced.

In my defense, my lack of appreciation for the complexities of business is akin to the common human trait of underestimating the complexity of any activity with which we have had little experience, whether it's being a good gardener or a good government servant. In my case, I backed into the idea of starting a company out of frustration rather than operating from a more positive motivation. Recall that only after I failed as a warrior in taking on the MCC computer-aided design program did I seek funding for the research that is the basis of ETI's product line. The reason I pursued the project rather than simply find another programming or software management position is that I had enough experience to realize that too many aspects of these positions were distasteful to me. But the reason that I thought about starting a company to productize the results of the research was because I didn't see any point in doing the research unless somebody would benefit from it. (Perhaps this pragmatic bent is why I was a lousy academic.) But all the while I was talking about starting a company I had no idea what was involved in the process, and everyone knew it, starting with MCC management.

The only reason I believe that I succeeded with the spinout of the company from MCC, and with making it through the first four years, was my partnership with Robin Curle and the support received from Bob Inman. When we first met, Robin and I were almost polar opposites. As the daughter of a former VP at General Electric, Robin was grounded in business, and by the time we spun out from MCC she had fourteen years in software sales—twice at start-ups and once at a turnaround. (A turnaround is a company which has successfully recovered from a prolonged period of financial distress.) She was aggressive, self-confident, and optimistic. Although I was aggressive, I was insecure, not a little paranoid, and slow to trust. When she came to me in January 1990 and offered to assist me with the spinout, I welcomed the help but was uncertain about the person—who she was, what she valued, and what she wanted.

As it turned out, Robin was an outstanding partner. She helped recast the financials in the business plan so they looked less naive. She told me that I had to stop dressing like an academic and look the part of a CEO. (It was wonderful having an excuse to buy clothes.) Most important, she coached me on what to say and what not to say when talking to venture capitalists. I had to appear confident and strong and focus on describing the market opportunity and the value proposition to the customer rather than on the technical merits of our solution.

There had been three failed spinout attempts at MCC prior to ours. Either they never got sufficient internal support, or the research sponsors failed to license them the technology. (The sponsors funding the basic research didn't like the idea that someone else was going to make money off of it.) As a result, I took a somewhat different tack and attempted to demonstrate a groundswell of interest in forming a start-up. Thus, in January 1990, three weeks after my father died and one year after we had obtained the research funds for the project, we held a one-week workshop for our research sponsors. We demonstrated the prototypes we had developed and conducted labs in how to use them. The software was not stable, but it did illustrate how the architecture we proposed could solve the problems we were addressing. The last morning of the workshop, I asked Bob White, who was at that time the vice president of the Advanced Computing Technology program and now serves as the director of the Data Storage Systems Center at Carnegie-Mellon University, to come to the wrap-up session. I asked each of the seventeen attendees from the seven research sponsors four questions.

Do you think the architecture of the prototype could successfully solve the problem?

Would your company benefit from this technology if it were a supported product?

Is your company likely to take this technology to product within two years of the end of the project?

Would you have any problem if we tried to organize some collaborative means of getting the product to market?

The answers all came out as I had expected. Voilà! A groundswell. My research sponsors had chartered me to undertake a spinout.

While the sponsors' endorsement was sufficient to make MCC management discuss the topic with me, I encountered significant resistance. In fact, Grant Dove, the CEO of MCC, refused to meet with me and requested that I work through his staff until nine months after I started the spinout effort.[1] As a result, for the next nine months I met regularly with Tom Kirkland, MCC's general counsel; Bob White; and after Bob left to be undersecretary of commerce for technology, his replacement Les Belady. They kept me informed of the next round of objections, and then Robin and I would strategize about how to answer that round. There were some pretty intense internal battles, such as when a new boss under Les thought he would help with the spinout and inch his way into serving as CEO of the new venture.

MCC's chronic refrain throughout the period was "You can't do it." At first, they said, "You can't do it." Then it became "OK, OK, you can do it, but you can't work there," followed by "You can do it and you can work there, but you can't run it." We just kept our heads down and continued to answer the objections.

It took eleven months and four MCC board meetings, at which we were required to sit in the hall while one of Grant's staff presented, but we won final approval from the board in December 1990. We had given all seven corporate sponsors a chance to invest. We asked for a commitment of $200,000 a year from each sponsor for a period of two years. Five wanted to do it, three got it through their management chain, two found the money, and one wrote the check. The manager in that company concluded that he didn't want to take on the grief of justifying an equity position to his board and requested instead a five-year license to the product. By the time it was over, we had cut a deal in which MCC had a small amount of equity and a royalty relationship that capped out at $4 million. In turn, we had a license for the technology, equipment, furniture, and insurance from MCC (the cost for all of which we subsequently paid) and our seed money.

But getting out was only half the battle. After eight months of working with a broker to raise money, we were broke and had to put everyone on half pay or find contracting jobs for those who couldn't afford that kind of cut. At that time we began to look for a business angel and talked to Bob Inman among others. A former admiral in the Navy, Bob had served as director of the National Security Agency, deputy director of the CIA, and had been the original CEO of MCC. In approximately October 1990, six weeks after we talked to him and when our bank balance was $25,000, Bob offered to invest $250,000 at whatever price we could raise the money and wrote us a check on a handshake. Less than two months later we closed our first venture round with Menlo Ventures.

## Notes

1. To be fair to Grant, he had his hands full. By the time he had assumed the position of CEO, the shareholder companies were all facing financial challenges and were grumbling that they weren't sure that their investments in MCC were going to pay off. In that kind of climate, his primary responsibilities were keeping his shareholders satisfied and the money to fund operations coming in. Little wonder that he didn't want to be distracted by my one project.

# Chapter 2

# The Global Conflict
## Issues in Planning an Exit Strategy

Victory in warfare, like all success, is temporary. You can decimate your enemy's troops, storm their cities, loot, and pillage. You can even enjoy the spoils of war for the rest of your life, but ultimately times change, civilizations fall, and the victor becomes the victim. In today's volatile economy, investors tend to be impatient for the outcome, cutting their losses when a company fails to perform and cashing their check when it does. One of upper management's most important jobs is to make the right trade-off decisions to ensure that the company always has access to capital at a good price. As a result, one of the most important decisions the management of a private company makes is whether to take the company public, that is, to register it with the Securities and Exchange Commission (SEC) for the purpose of making its stock available to the general public for purchase.

## Why a Soldier Needs to Worry about the Scope of the War

Depending on the size of the company you work for, you may be more or less aware of what is happening on this front, even if you are a manager. If you have signed on to work at a venture-backed start-up, your expectation is that the company will undertake an initial public offering. The decision to take a company public depends on many factors. If some particular type of stock is hot—like those for companies based on the Internet or on biotechnology—and the company has experienced sufficient revenue growth to show promise, the company may choose to go public even when it is still showing losses because the public market is paying large multiples with no penalty for a lack of profitability. Likewise, if the venture investors need to cash out and stocks in the company's market space are currently faring well in the public market, management may decide to dress the company up for an IPO as quickly as possible, for example, by cutting expenses and targeting a new hot area of substantial growth. In any case, this decision is likely to have a profound impact, good or bad, on you as an employee. If the company is a wild success like Microsoft or Dell and you are an early employee, you may become wealthy. On the other hand, if the company fails to perform after the offering, you may find yourself holding stock that nobody wants to buy.

Working for a private company is no less risky. If you work for a company that is not considering a public offering, either because it is not exhibiting sufficient growth potential or because the owners do not want to deal with the overhead of running a public company, you must assess the likelihood or timing of a sale and its impact on your job security. Large private companies, such as Cargill (one of the oldest and largest private companies in the U.S.) and SAIC (which runs its own internal stock exchange for employees), have thrived for decades. But more often, at some point the owners want liquidity, and depending on the type of business it is, the resulting transaction could mean a drastic transition for the employees.

In a small company, it is relatively easy to determine how the company is faring generally—for example, observe whether you are hiring new employees, acquiring new office space, or signing on large numbers of customers—but unless management decides to share the financials, you will not be privy to the economic health of the organization. If the company has raised a large amount of venture capital, it can spend like a sailor while generating little or no revenue. In the case of a public company, you can access the financials, but because of the way the numbers are reported, determining how well your particular area of the business is doing may not be easy. If a particular area of the business is not profitable, the company may decide to divest itself of that part of the business (as in the case of Texas Instruments selling its software business to Sterling Software) or do away with it altogether (as in the case of Control Data and its supercomputer subsidiary). In either instance, many people lost their jobs.

It is often not possible for soldiers to concentrate on defending the beachhead in front of them while worrying about whether the enemy is going to attack their flank. To win the battle they must count on the perspective and judgment of their commanding officers and the skill and courage of their colleagues. However, because war in business rarely involves life and death, management and employees consider the results of losing battles less serious. Therefore, as a soldier you must develop the instincts to assess the health and potential future of the organization you work for. You may choose to remain in a risky situation because you like the job and the product—and if it will be easy for you to find a comparable job—but the choice should be yours. In this chapter, we will look at the two major classes of transaction—going public and mergers or acquisitions—and the ways they affect a company to help you make your own assessment of your company's ability to thrive on the corporate battlefield.

## Taking the Battle Global through an IPO

Venture capitalists look for entrepreneurs who understand the importance of planning for the right kind of exit strategy. For the investor to get a maximum return on his or her investment, the company usually needs to exhibit a history of strong growth in both revenue and profits. There are occasional exceptions, such as in the area of biotech or Internet companies, where the promise of some technology can sometimes lead to huge market caps (a figure computed by multiplying the price per share by the number of shares outstanding) even when the company does not yet have revenues. Most companies, however, must demonstrate a solid history of growth in revenues and profit for shareholders to receive the best return on their investment, regardless of the exit strategy.

Companies typically choose to go public if they need capital, have exhibited strong growth, and believe that they have the potential to continue such growth as an independent entity for some time. Going public provides investors and employees with a means of cashing in their shares of stock, and because the amount of capital in the public market is significantly greater than among private equity investors, the company is more likely to be able to raise additional money at a better price. However, a number of problems associated with being a public company can ultimately make it harder to run the business and for founders or employees with a large number of shares to cash out.

## New Rules of Engagement

A private company can be run like a guerrilla war, opportunistically and stealthily, with few engagements involving large numbers or an open field. Running a public company requires significantly more control since the generals must publish a plan of attack and most engagements take place in an open field. In short, there are more constraints on running a public company. Most of these constraints result from the SEC's attempt to protect the public investor from being defrauded. The assumption is that investors in private companies are knowledgeable and responsible for ascertaining for themselves whether the company is being run responsibly. Some aspects of a company's accounting, for example, computing tax liability or payroll taxes, are a matter of law and general accounting principles. Other features—for example, whether to count the annual maintenance fee paid by customers for ongoing support as service or product revenue—are not important unless the company is entertaining the possibility of going public.

The SEC develops and maintains these accounting guidelines to help the investors in a public company understand how the company is performing financially by allowing them to compare the companies' published financials to those of other public companies in the same industry. Many of these guidelines have been developed because of abuses in the past. For example, one area of particular concern in the software industry is revenue recognition, or the question of when the company has actually sold a product to a client. This topic first became critical when several software companies allowed customers to sign a license that contained a return clause or wherever there was a "side" letter from the salesperson or customer permitting the return of the product. In these cases, because there was no actual commitment being made, it was relatively easy for salesmen to obtain signatures, and the companies in question reported the figures reflected in these licenses as revenue for the quarter. As a result, the investor had the impression that the companies in question were making more money than they actually were.

In an effort to eliminate this abuse, subsequent SEC guidelines prohibit a software company from recognizing the revenue unless the product has been delivered, and cannot be returned, and all material services associated with the contract have been performed (or the portion of the revenue associated with the services has been deferred). Savvy investors also look at such things as days sales outstanding (DSOs), which refer to the average length of time between the sale and the time that the company collects the money from the customer, to determine whether the software company is writing "clean" business. Other industries are constrained by similar accounting guidelines.

The management of a public company faces an additional set of risks because they must publish their financial results quarterly. Based on the performance indicated by these results, large stockholders may rush to buy or sell large volumes of stock, driving the price up or down. If the stock price falls significantly, it becomes hard for a company to raise more capital by selling additional stock or bonds.

Even more important in these litigious times, if a company fails to perform at or ahead of the financial analysts' expectations, it runs the risk of a shareholder class action suit. In fact, there are law firms where partners watch for just such surprises in financial performance since they can file a class action lawsuit on behalf of the owner of a single share of stock. Even if a company's management is totally above reproach, the cost associated with defending the company against a class action suit can be prohibitive. As a result, public companies carry director and officer insurance, which protects the directors and officers of companies from personal liability in the case of such a suit. Consequently, unless the potential damage is so prohibitive, as in the suits against the tobacco companies or the makers of breast implants, the company usually tries to settle rather than going to court. (Part of their reason for settling is their lack of faith in the jury system, where they perceive a near knee-jerk reaction in favor of the individual at the expense of an organization.) In fact, this tendency to settle out of court is so pronounced that one of the lawyers preying on the software industry has been quoted as saying, "The D&O insurance is always mine. The only question is whether I can get anything out of the company itself."

Because of this liability, public companies have strict rules regarding who can speak to the press regarding certain issues. In the early days of being public, the CEO and chief financial officer (CFO) are typically the only two individuals who speak to the press, financial analysts, and large investors regarding the company's business performance. These individuals are typically trained not to make forward predictions about revenue or profit, or they run the risk of being accused of misleading the market. In larger companies, to shield the CEO, one or more individuals in charge of investor relations assist the CFO. As a result, one of the largest challenges faced by a public company is how to keep the financial analysts sufficiently informed about the business, without actually quoting figures, so that their predictions closely coincide with the company's actual performance. Private communications between the company and the analysts regarding this information are called "whisper" numbers.

Recently Congress has tried to cap the punitive damages that can be awarded through class action suits and pass "safe harbor" laws to allow a company to talk more openly about the potential for revenues and profits without making them liable. The former didn't pass, however. With telecommunications, the press, and today's sound bite mentality, it is probably political suicide to try to protect business at the expense of an individual's chance to win big in court. Likewise, safe harbor laws help, but do not eliminate the problem of avoiding litigation.

## Engaging Mercenaries

Despite the risks, in a strong market solid companies—particularly those with venture capitalists as investors—will choose an IPO over a merger or acquisition as the liquidity event of choice. The act of going public takes anywhere from three to six months and involves two types of organizations—investment bankers and public investors.

### Investment Bankers

Investment bankers are like the leaders of groups of mercenaries. These leaders exhibit exceptional skills in a particular type of warfare and will serve the company well by supplying a steady stream of investors as long as they stand to profit from it. They are responsible for representing appropriate candidates to the investor in the public market and handling the planning and execution of the transaction, including setting the stock's price at the offering. In addition to handling equity (stock) transactions, these bankers also help companies do such things as issue bonds, manage capital, and execute mergers and acquisitions. In a public offering, they make their money by charging the company a fee and by charging a small handling fee on each sale or purchase. Investment bankers differ predominantly in terms of the class of investors they serve. Some deal only with large investors. *Bulge* firms have access to large amounts of capital, and *boutique* firms focus on providing expert coverage of particular industries. Both of these firms target large individual or institutional investors. *Retail* bankers support the large numbers of required transactions for small individual investors.

In handling a public offering, the investment banker has three responsibilities:

- to perform sufficient due diligence on the company and its previous performance to represent its worthiness in the transaction,

- to provide the company with a venue for introducing it to key investors so the company can obtain a reasonable price on the offering, and

- to present its long-term clients with promising investment opportunities.

Note that there is an inherent conflict between the last two responsibilities. For the investor to make a good return, the price of the company's stock must go up over time, and in fact, part of the hype around hot IPOs is that the stock price can rise significantly in a relatively short period. As a result, the challenge for the banker—and the area where the company making the offering sometimes disagrees—is what constitutes a good price at the offering. On the one hand, because the offering price determines how much cash the company will actually get (less expenses and the bankers' fees), the company tends to favor a higher price than the banker. On the other hand, if the price obtained is too high, even the company is hurt. Unless the company significantly outperforms predictions, which rarely happens, a high price can reduce the investors' return after the offering.

## Investors

Investors tend to fall into one of three categories: large individual or institutional investors, individual investors, and the newest on the scene, day traders. Institutional investors are just that—a group that invests money for some larger entity, such as a bank or a pension fund. Bulge and boutique firms tend to focus on institutional or large private investors because of the larger transactions these investors typically make. When taking their case to the company making the offering, these bankers argue that their long-term relationship with these large investors helps them "make a market for the stock." Retail bankers, on the other hand, argue that the large transactions made by institutional investors can contribute to extreme swings in stock value and that a small company benefits from having a sizable amount of stock spread across a significantly larger number of retail customers. The day trader is an individual who uses the Internet to monitor and maintain his own portfolio, capitalizing on short-term swings in the marketplace.

Note two forces are at work that may dramatically change the way investment bankers deal with both companies and investors—the deregulation of the banking industry and the arrival of the day trader. Up until recently commercial banks like Wells Fargo or Bank One could not offer mutual funds or initiate public offerings. With the greater latitude afforded by the new regulations, banks are acquiring or merging with the established institutions in that marketplace. As a result, many of the most prestigious boutique banks, such as Alex Brown, Robertson Stephens, and Hambrecht & Quist, have been acquired by large commercial banks. Whether the bank will seek to change the focus and skills of its investment banking over time remains to be seen. Similarly, the impact of the day trader—coupled with electronic trades, which are triggered automatically when a particular condition is hit—may make the market even more volatile than the days when the bulk of trading in a particular stock was in the hands of large private or institutional investors and a bulge banker could influence the market simply by giving personal advice. In any case, these factors plus the globalization of financial markets make the trends of the future anybody's guess.

## The IPO Battle Plan

Just as mercenaries look for potentially lucrative conflicts, investment bankers are constantly looking for hot private companies to take public. As a result, if a company is growing aggressively in a large market and has received any national attention, it can expect numerous investment bankers to come calling. If the company wants to go public, it should take advantage of these opportunities to build these relationships well before the transaction for a number of reasons:

- to educate the bankers about its marketspace,

- to understand how the bankers cover that space because visibility is critical for maintaining interest in the stock once the offering is complete, and

- to give the bankers time to learn about the company so that when the company is ready to file they know that its records are not filled with "revisionist" history.

## The Bankers and Cutting the Deal

Once the company and its investors have determined that the company is ready to initiate a public offering, the company invites four to eight of the potential investment bankers to pitch their business. At this point in the transaction, the bankers are selling. Since the fees for handling an IPO are fairly standard, management must consider the following when choosing their bankers:

- whether their financial analysts already follow the comparable companies and, if so, how well regarded is the analyst in question;

- the amount and types of capital each banker manages, for example, whether it is international or regional, focuses on retail or institutional investors, and so on; and

- whether the company's projected revenue growth is sufficiently large to remain of interest to the banker after the transaction.

## Due Diligence, the All Hands Meeting, and the Quiet Period

Once the bankers have been chosen and the deal cut, the bankers' due diligence begins. At this point, an "all hands" meeting is called for the bankers, the company's management, the legal representatives of both, and the company's accounting firm to review the company's position. One of the banker's primary responsibilities in underwriting the offering is to assure the public investor that the company is representing itself accurately. The bankers and company representatives then draft the S-1, or the text of the prospectus used to describe the offering. In addition to detailing the company's business and growth potential, much of this document is formulaic and geared to pointing out the risk factors associated with the investment. Because there is a fine line between selling the company's prospects and protecting the public's interest, this drafting period can take a considerable amount of time. During this interval, it is critical that the company maintain a quiet period in which it does nothing out of the ordinary to tout its business. Otherwise, it could be charged with trying to unfairly influence the value of its stock at the offering.

Once the S-1 is complete, it is filed with the Securities Exchange Commission for review. The SEC's charter is to enforce and ensure that any company offering securities in the public market is in compliance with their regulations. The SEC has thirty days with which to submit questions or comments. If the SEC raises any questions about the S-1, the company has thirty days in which to respond. Once the SEC approves the S-1, the company prints a copy of the prospectus—excluding the stock price—exactly as it will accompany the offering. This document is used in conjunction with the roadshow to determine at what price the stock will be offered to the public market.

## The Roadshow

While the SEC is reviewing the S-1, the company and bankers hold a series of roadshow preparation sessions. The roadshow is the primary means by which the investment bankers introduce the company to large investors and get the feedback they need to determine at what price the stock should be offered. The lead banker is responsible for setting up the roadshow and chooses presentation sites in anywhere from five to fifteen cities, possibly in different countries, depending on the size of the deal and the potential interest of the investors in the market. In each city, institutional investors and large private investors are invited to a series of meetings so they can hear about the offering directly from the company's management. Because most of these meetings typically run no longer than an hour or two and because in an active market these investors can see up to thirty or forty IPO opportunities in a month, the company's presentation must be crisp and convincing.

Once the roadshow is over, the lead investor makes the "book" by calling the attendees to gauge their potential interest in the stock and by asking them what amount they might be interested in and at what price. These quotes do not represent commitment on the potential investor's part and therefore cannot be taken at face value, particularly because no one names his maximum price to a seller. However, after querying all of the roadshow attendees, if the book is oversubscribed—that is, the total amount of stock "committed" to is greater than the amount being sold—then a higher price for the stock is favored.

## Pricing

The day before the offering, the company's management and the bankers meet to set the price of the stock. This discussion is frequently heated, as it is typical for the bankers to want a lower price than the company. This disagreement is not unlike those between the company and its venture investors about the best kind of exit strategy. The investment banker's long-term customers are its investors, and as a result, their ultimate commitment in executing an IPO is to ensure that any of their investors who purchase stock in the offering get a good return on their investment. To realize such returns, the stock price must go up after the offering. To the extent that a 120-day lockup prevents private investors, founders, or employees from selling their stock, it is also in the company's best interest that the stock not be overvalued on the offering. However, determining what is fair value versus what is "overvalued" is precisely what leads to disagreements.

## Survival on the Global Battlefield

As discussed earlier, taking a company public places a whole new set of constraints on running the business, the most pressing of which is having to justify the company's financial performance on a quarterly basis. (Private companies commonly provide their board with financials outlining performance on a quarterly basis, but rarely do they give these numbers to all shareholders, much less make them a matter of public record.) Not only must the public company file its financials for public scrutiny every quarter, but it must justify why it over- or under-performed and, in so doing, keep the financial analysts' faith in the business, the management, and the market for its goods or services. While institutional and large private investors in public companies may be sophisticated investors, they usually do not have direct experience with the company's management on day-to-day operational issues. As a result, they tend to consider a company a purely financial instrument and rely heavily on what the financial analysts predict about the company's performance. The CEO or CFO typically holds a series of calls or meetings after each quarter to answer questions about the company's performance.

Based on perceptions of how the company is doing, the banker's financial analyst determines whether the investor should buy (that is, the company's prospects look outstanding), hold (you don't have to unload immediately, but things could get dicey), or sell (you should have sold when I said "hold"). The banks typically reward their financial analysts based on the success of their predictions. As a result, if an analyst is caught up short or seriously surprised (even if positively) by a company's performance, he or she can be a long time in forgiving the company and, if the company is small enough, even stop covering its stock. The latter action can effectively eliminate the market for the stock. If no bank covers the stock, then it becomes harder for the company to seem newsworthy and get any coverage. As a result, the only people who are paying attention are the individuals and institutions that already own stock. Without any market pressure driving up the price per share, the stock's value will languish, seriously compromising the company's ability to raise money.

## The Spoils of War

Working at a company when it executes an initial public offering can be exhilarating. Employees finally have some extrinsic proof of the value of what they have helped bring to the marketplace and, after the lockout period, an opportunity to reap a cash reward above and beyond their salary. Likewise, even if you are hired after it's public, it can be equally exciting to be an employee of the company as long as it continues to grow and reap a great deal of positive publicity. Companies have long used employee stock option plans as a way of sharing the company's good fortune and of building solidarity within the workforce. It used to be the case that if you stayed with a strong public company over a long period of time and exercised your options, you could have amassed a considerable sum by the time you retired. For example, my father started working as a pharmaceutical representative for Eaton Laboratories in the 1950s and retired from the same company—by that time, Morton Thiokol—forty years later with his stock worth more than $1 million.

## Those Spoiled by War

Times have changed. Although employees of successful companies may wind up as millionaires, it's usually after a considerably shorter tenure. This telescoping of time, and the fact that a stock's worth is less tied to profits than it used to be, makes banking on the worth of your options a much riskier proposition. Solid performance alone is not enough to ensure a steady or rising stock price.

Consider the case of Dr. L, who bootstrapped his software company to $1 million in revenues with no external funding. Dr. L's technology performed source code analysis and was of wide benefit to the information technology (IT) organizations within Fortune 5000 companies. Seeking to choose a vertical market to facilitate the penetration of his product, Dr. L hit on the year 2000 (Y2K) problem as a market with significant pull for his technology. After establishing a strong growth record, he took his company public, and it continued to grow at the rate of 200 percent over the next year with 25 percent profits. However, because the financial analysts determined that software companies addressing the Y2K problem would face diminishing markets by the last half of 1999, they began downgrading the growth potential of these stocks in the first half of 1998. As a result, Dr. L's stock price dropped precipitously, despite the fact that his company was continuing to grow at an aggressive rate and that his product had significant value for other applications. As a result, he could not receive fair value on his own equity in selling his stock, and he faced an uphill battle in new marketing efforts because he had to try to turn around the analysts when they were more interested in following hot new companies than in reversing their judgment on one they had written off. In the end, rather than reaping the rewards for developing an excellent product, serving a strong market need, and building a sound business, most of Dr. L's net worth was tied up in stock he couldn't sell in a company with a set of unhappy employees and shareholders.

## Strength through Alliances: Mergers and Acquisitions (M&A)

Frequently companies look for some other way of achieving liquidity or ramping up their revenues beyond organic growth, namely, through mergers or acquisitions. Companies use all sorts of combinations. A private company can be acquired by either a private or public company, two public companies can merge or one acquire the other, or multiple companies merge at roughly the same time in a "rollup" to gain sufficient momentum for a public offering. In every case, the goal is to show almost immediate revenue growth by combining revenue streams, with the opportunity to improve profitability by cutting duplicate resources. In other words, the aftermath of any M&A event usually includes some downsizing.

Whether it's the short-term attitude of today's investor, the telescoping of time, or increased competition due to technological advances, mergers and acquisitions are definitely a major force in today's economy. Mergerstat®[1] reported that the aggregate deal value for mergers and acquisitions in 1999 exceeded $1.12 trillion without the MCI Worldcom/Sprint deal, which was valued at $129 billion. In 1998, the aggregate value was a record $1.19 trillion, when ten of the largest mergers and acquisitions in history were announced.

This activity reflects the significant consolidation taking place in banking in the United States (and to a lesser extent in Europe), accompanied by changes in regulation that are making banking, insurance, and securities businesses converge. Likewise, changes in regulation and fierce competition to become established in the Internet market have led to significant consolidation in the telecommunications industry. Finally, more cross-border transactions, like the 1999 deals between British Petroleum and Amoco and between Daimler-Benz and Chrysler, are taking place.

To the stockholders of a private company, an acquisition can be good or bad. If the company has performed well and is acquired at the right price by a strong public company—for example, as in our previous example of Tivoli Systems, which was acquired by IBM in 1996 for $743 million—it can mean liquidity at a more or less guaranteed price. If the private company has not performed well, however, the shareholders will get liquidity at a significantly lower price than they had hoped for, and in the worst case, the company will be acquired by another company that is not strong and is trying to use the acquisition to boost its own low stock value. In this last case, it may take years before major stockholders from the acquired company can cash out or, if the acquiring company doesn't pull off the desired turnaround, it may take yet another acquisition by some larger entity.

In either a merger or acquisition, the employee runs two risks—the possibility of being redundant (as the British put it) and subsequently laid off or the possibility of simply being miserable after a change in cultures. While most of us would argue that our salary is one of the most important reasons why we work, in actuality our career decisions are rarely driven entirely by financial rewards. Rather we want work that we consider valuable and interesting, where both our contribution is recognized and our coworkers share our values. And herein lies the rub for the employee whose company is acquired or merged, for companies, like people, have values and personality. Walmart, for example, is legendary for its value system—its rigorous policies for minimizing the cost of merchandising while demonstrating the importance of the customer by having "greeters" and so forth. While this environment might be ideal for some individuals, it allows little room for creativity. Individuals who might thrive in a smaller retail environment, where they could focus on attractive merchandise displays and personalized service for customers, may feel totally thwarted in the Walmart environment.

## Spoils or Spoiled? Uncertain Outcomes

Some acquisitions, like that of Tivoli, are a clear success for everyone involved. But for every great success, hundreds, if not thousands, of stories end quite differently. For example, one entrepreneur I know, whom we will call Bill, was part of a company with a software product that was probably the best of the breed. A larger company with revenues of $275 million acquired Bill's company (for a little over $6 million) and another slightly larger vendor offering the same type of product in order to own the market. The intent was to simply kill off the best product and use the other more established product as the base for moving forward.

Bill, who had been the architect for the product selected for extinction, left the company and several years later wound up at another public software company as its chief architect on a new, superior version of the same type of product. Just as it came to market, the very same company that acquired Bill's first venture bought the company for which he had gone to work. Needless to say Bill was far from satisfied with his return on his sweat equity.

However, just as there are variable results with IPOs, it is often hard to predict the results of an acquisition on the basis of the transaction itself. Sometimes what at first might appear a failure turns out be a very lucky move. For example, a start-up in Austin developed some excellent software for handheld devices but found its growth limited since only a handful of vendors could serve as its potential customers. As a result, the company decided to sell itself, but because the potential buyers knew that only one or two competitors were bidding, the company sold for a disappointing price. Shortly afterward, however, the purchasing company was itself acquired for a much stronger price—in part because of its bargain acquisition—by a public company whose stock value has increased significantly since the transaction.

## What This Battle Means for the Workplace Warrior

We have spent a considerable amount of time on workplace warfare at the macro-level, that is, from upper management's point of view. Understanding the enemies and struggles they face can help you as a potential warrior determine the importance of the battles you want to take on. To thrive, all companies must succeed on two planes—that of offering value to the customer and that of offering value to the shareholder. Unless both constituencies are satisfied, trouble will follow. In picking your battles within an organization, you should gauge the importance of what you are fighting for in terms of its potential significance to the company, and to do that you must appreciate your battle's impact on the outcome of the CEO's war. For example, when I was at Texas Instruments, I considered management's decision to keep their differentiating technology, such as speech and natural language, proprietary to the TI personal computer as terrible a mistake as making the hardware incompatible with the IBM PC. But in the scheme of things and the company's legacy—a history of success based on being one of the few vendors manufacturing proprietary technology— the business I was arguing for was small potatoes. Likewise, in late 1998, at ETI a key technical person left because we didn't have an Internet strategy. We were not generating sufficient growth in revenue to fund the then-current business model and didn't have the resources—or the ability (at that time) to raise capital—to allow us to pursue a new market. Today our situation has changed, and we are currently raising funds to take our key competency into the Internet space.

In short, regardless of whether you are right, if the beachhead you're bent on taking is not critical to the war's outcome or upper management does not acknowledge its importance or cannot act on it at the time, your battle might be fruitless. You may learn a lot in fighting the fight, provided that you are even given the ammunition or troops to succeed, but neither you nor your company are likely to reap financial benefits from your success.

## Notes

1. Mergerstat® is the mergers and acquisitions research division of Houlihan Lokey Howard & Zukin, a national investment banking firm. Businesspeople use it to help assess the impact of an M&A transaction.

# section II

# Basic
# Training

# Chapter 3

# Mastery of Weapons
## Effective Communication in the Workplace

n the workplace, words and wit are the weapons of choice. Just as a good martial artist anticipates an opponent's move, to be effective on the job you must be able to hear beyond the words and understand not just the immediate meaning but why an individual voices a particular set of opinions. Paying attention to what people say in various situations can give you a good sense of their motivation, heart, and vulnerability. However, to be effective in battle, you must be equally aware of your own meaning, strengths, and vulnerabilities. This chapter discusses common behavior found in the workplace and the conversational clues that indicate how an individual would behave as an ally or an enemy as well as his capacity for growth or leadership.

Before we discuss different corporate climates for communication and common types of conversational behavior and what they can mean, I would like to take a few moments—retired linguist that I am—to consider how rich and complex a medium language is. The fact that children learn language with little or no formal instruction has long been a topic of interest among linguists and psychologists, leading them to suggest that the human brain is somehow wired for language. This idea is even more interesting in light of the fact that no one can identify similarities in spectrograms, or graphs of the sound waves produced in speech. In other words, spectograms of different people saying the same words show no common element, yet we consistently recognize the sounds as being the same. What's even more amazing is that so often what we say is not what we mean, but it is not because we are being duplicitous. For example, if a couple is at a party and the wife says to her husband, "It's getting pretty late," she is not making an observation but an implied suggestion. Likewise, the question "Are you going to take the garbage out?" expects an action and not a response of "yes" or "no." In short, over the years we acquire a set of conventions for how we express certain desires and intents. Add this indirectness to an approved corporate communication style and an individual's psychological motives, intentional or unintentional, and you see that trying to understand what a person is really saying can take a fair amount of analysis.

## Styles of Corporate Communication

Forty or fifty years ago, communication skills in the workplace were not as crucial as they are today. Fast, accurate work was sufficient for the assembly line, but in the information age, good speaking and writing skills are essential. In fact, depending on the company you work for, a particular style of communication may be required. However, the style that serves you well in one environment within a company may do you serious damage in another. For example, in 1998 we hired an extremely bright and experienced woman to run our marketing department. Although P looked very young, she actually had fourteen years of marketing experience at a large Fortune 1000-size electronics manufacturer, where she was one of few women to reach the level of director. Because of its size and hard-hitting male environment, P had trained herself to prepare thoroughly and to present briskly, almost daring anyone to question her competence. While this style had always served her well in her previous position, it initially alienated a good number of us at our small, consensus-oriented company.

Sales personnel in electronics firms are usually fairly technical but have a more straightforward sales cycle than in large solution software sales. The manufacturer buying their component has certain requirements and the sale is typically tied to the best cost-performance trade-off the company can make. In the big-ticket software business, the sales cycle is very different. We sell a software package—the average license agreement is more than $200,000—to companies undertaking strategic initiatives, such as coping with a merger or acquisition, modifying their business to accommodate changes in regulation, or implementing a new set of applications or hardware/software platform. In such a solution sale, the salesperson needs to understand the customer's problems and concerns, whether they are technical, political, or procedural. As a result, our successful salesmen become quite knowledgeable about the forces at play in the market. Yet when our sales personnel tried to share some of their insights with P, she was often resistant, saying that marketing was her job and that she felt confident she could do it. Her attitude struck the salespeople as arrogant and created hard feelings.

A company may also favor different types of communication styles among different groups, for example, adversarial and outspoken among engineers but formal and dispassionate among the executives. Sometimes the style is dictated by the responsibilities of the employee's position. For instance, in a public company the CEO and CFO must respond in real-time to questions from investors and the press about a quarter's performance. In doing so, they must balance a desire to speak favorably about the company's prospects with the knowledge that any overstatement could later lead to unfavorable treatment by financial analysts or even litigation by shareholders who feel they have been misled.

## Management Misspeak

The most common complaints among employees are that management decisions simply don't make sense and that management—or the press, the president, almost anybody—is brain-dead. While it may be emotionally gratifying to make such judgments, as an employee with a vested interest not only in your career but also in the health of the company you work for, you need to understand exactly why you disagree with a particular manager. Is he plainly wrong? Is he being manipulative? Or does he simply lack the necessary communication skills to lead effectively?

### Obsolescence

As companies grow and their businesses change, bad decisions may be due to management obsolescence. For example, in the 1980s, before much of the corporate downsizing, one often met managers who had been with a company for fifteen or twenty years and whose hands-on experience with the company no longer pertained to the company's then-current products. As a result, their instincts and assumptions could lead the company to make significant errors. For instance, the initial success of Texas Instruments was based on the integrated circuit and chip technology. Its focus was on efficiently manufacturing of a quality product, which was available from a handful of vendors, and on selling business that could be won on the strict price-performance of the hardware. As TI moved into computers, it assumed that the same parameters would hold; however, people buying computers don't care as much about an ergonomic keyboard or the amount of silicon real estate on a chip as about what the machines can do. Focusing on the hardware's power, TI originally decided to make its personal computer incompatible with the IBM-PC, thinking that better ergonomics and superior graphics would lead the consumer to abandon IBM. If customers based their decisions purely on hardware performance, they would have bought the TI PC, but because it could not run the more than 10,000 software products available for the IBM PC, the TI PC was a bust. TI eventually revisited their decision and made its PC IBM-compatible, but the company had already missed the market window.

TI's executive management made the mistake of assuming that the same parameters that applied to the semiconductor industry could apply to computers and software. However, while some companies' bad decisions can be blamed on managerial obsolescence, more often the case in business is that a decision is not bad, just poorly communicated. Too frequently, skills in leadership and communication are not emphasized as much as they should be when determining who should be promoted to management and how they should be trained. Many employees are promoted to management either because they are extremely talented at some aspect of the business or they are good at "selling" their superiors, but that skill does not mean that they understand human nature or how to motivate people. As a result, they often cannot explain business decisions so that they make sense to their employees. Some common mistakes that managers make when communicating with their employees follow.

### Treating Information as Power

Managers who are either insecure in their own skills or who play politics frequently treat company information as a secret weapon. They figure that as long as they keep this information to themselves they don't have to worry about any of their colleagues or subordinates showing them up. Rather than seeking to explain what they know, they exchange the minimum amount of information required to obtain the behavior that they believe will help them or, to be more charitable, make the company successful. I once had a manager working for me who was driven by his compensation. Since a significant portion of his compensation came from a quarterly bonus based on the financial performance of his department, he tended to set his priorities in terms of what maximized his group's profitability. He therefore filtered information—both up and down—that would influence others to support decisions that reinforced his goals. Otherwise, he was an extremely talented manager, who excelled at hiring strong leaders to work under him. His downfall came when two of his senior managers became frustrated with the company's failure to act on several good suggestions they had made. When they discovered that their suggestions had never made it to my desk, the team lost faith in his ability to carry out the primary responsibility of a manager—to act as an accurate and effective communicator of important information both up and down.

## Failing to Understand the Business

We discussed what can happen when management's assumptions about the business no longer hold. But sometimes new managers or middle managers simply do not understand the business and, therefore, cannot be good interpreters of corporate direction. Because they simply do not have the background, they often miss the point of what upper management presents to them. For example, when I first served as a manager of TI, the president of the Digital Systems Group held an employee meeting on a quarterly basis in the cafeteria to discuss the company's performance as well as general economic factors affecting the business. As a transplanted academic only two years into the business world who had avoided following financial and economic news (in part, in defiance and fear of turning into my father, who did very little with his free time but read such material and compute and recompute his net worth), I found these meetings a total waste of time. And yet I was one of the loudest critics of the company's mistakes in my area. I was correct about most of these mistakes, but my frustration with upper management would have been significantly less if I had realized how relatively unimportant software and computer revenue was to TI.

Frequently, a manager's failure to understand corporate directives is less a matter of incompetence than a fear of asking questions. Most of us are afraid that we don't deserve the praise or recognition that we get and worry that eventually people will see our limitations. As a result, new or middle managers often don't press their bosses for details when discussing strategy; therefore, they do not have a complete picture to pass on to their employees.

### Failing to Understand Their Employees and How to Communicate with Them

Finally, even managers who understand and are committed to their company's vision sometimes have trouble conveying information effectively because they are not able to put themselves in their employees' place and give them the data they want. Great orators have the ability to anticipate the assumptions and reactions of their audience and to write and deliver their speeches in such a way as to lead their listeners to specific conclusions. Instead, too often, managers simply repeat what they have been told, perhaps adding their own spin but without addressing what their employees care about most, what they are likely to know, and what they fear. While every employee is different, there are often important similarities among the people working in functional areas that, if understood, help a manager determine what his employees need and want to know.

The software industry is a good example of a business where various functional groups have very different backgrounds and needs. Although most people who work for software companies are relatively well paid and are well informed about business and their company's market space, they frequently have widely divergent skills and concerns. For example, while both the people in sales and the programmers in development care equally about the company's financial performance, the information about product direction that they need in order to feel comfortable with the company's decisions differs significantly. To be successful, software salespeople must understand their customers' problems and how their software provides a solution. Because most new releases have additional features that will make selling the product easier, the salespeople are always eager to hear how closely the company is tracking to the promised delivery date. When the company is at risk of not making this date, the salespeople want to know why, but they typically don't need a detailed explanation, in part because they don't have the technical background required to follow it. Instead, they feel more comfortable with some high-level sense of what the problem is and how much longer it will take, or what new features must be sacrificed, to keep to the original delivery schedule. On the contrary, when talking about the same topic, programmers will delve into as much technical detail as possible.

One of the best technical managers that ever worked for me had exactly this problem. Technically, F was the smartest person I knew in the software field. As a result, I trusted him to manage multiple complex projects and felt comfortable both that any design decision made with the group was sound and that any trade-off made to keep a delivery date was reasonable. However, although many of the technical people he managed respected his technical expertise, they didn't feel comfortable working for him and felt that he was not totally honest with me because the company appeared to be ignoring their concerns. While F understood the business reasons driving the company to release a particular product within a certain timeframe, he didn't take enough time to ensure his people understood these issues. Likewise, when F made a trade-off decision, he didn't allot enough time for the group's members to express all their concerns about why the trade-off might not work. F was smart enough to explain to them how it could work, but because he didn't, his staff members developed nagging doubts that made them anxious about their potential success.

## If Your Manager Is a Poor Communicator

If you don't understand your manager, you can often work around it or even sometimes benefit from it. There are two tactics you can apply to this situation. First, become proactive and discover what you need to know about the company you work for, and second, try to determine why your manager is not effectively communicating.

### Arm Yourself with Knowledge

It is always important that you understand, to the best of your ability, the trade-offs made by the company you work for. If your manager can't explain them to you, look for other means of understanding how the business is being run. Ask someone in the marketing department for industry analysts' reports on your company and its products. If you work for a public company, you can obtain the financials from each quarterly filing and reports from the investment banking firms that follow the company's stock either from the Internet or a stockbroker. You don't have to learn to read the financials in detail, but look at patterns of revenue growth and profit as well as changes in the revenue mix. For example, if the company's financial growth is slowing and the amount of business being generated from international sources is growing significantly faster than that in the United States, you might ask yourself the following questions:

- Has the company saturated the U.S. marketplace, suggesting that in a number of years a similar thing will happen in the international marketplace?
- Is a different competitive dynamic working in the United States than elsewhere?

■ Does the company have a strategy for strengthening its business in the United States? For example, are new products or services being developed that might reinvigorate domestic growth?

### Use This Information to Understand Your Manager Better

Once you have armed yourself with a little information, ask your manager and other people in various departments within the company questions, but approach this task in a nonthreatening way. Ask as if you are interested and concerned that the right decisions have been made rather than implying that management is stupid or irresponsible. Don't ask a specific, detailed question about the company's financial performance or market strategy until you have ascertained that the person you are talking to is aware of this information. Otherwise, you might make the other person feel stupid or ill-informed, which could affect his attitude toward you, particularly if he is in a senior position. If your manager cannot answer such questions or is reluctant to answer them, then it is likely that either he or she considers information to be power or is just clueless about the business.

If your manager simply doesn't understand his audience, this kind of dialogue with your manager will likely be quite productive. You may realize that he does have much of the information you want if you simply ask for it, and by having done your own homework, you can determine whether his or her information is accurate. Likewise, your questions may lead the manager to understand that people want to know this kind of information and to adjust his or her style accordingly. However, even if the manager doesn't improve his style, your ability to articulate why the company is heading in a particular direction can be beneficial if you share this information with your colleagues when they express concern. If done with the right attitude, sharing this information can help make you a leader in your work group, which a good manager will reward by giving you greater responsibility, that is, as long as you continue to complete your assigned tasks in a timely and professional manner. (Trust me, no manager appreciates an employee who spends her time acting as a confessor instead of doing her work.)

## Be Proactive

In my own case, much of my professional dissatisfaction resulted from not doing the kind of research I suggest above. While teaching at Washington State University and later when working at TI, I complained about seemingly stupid policies, but I understood little about the economic environment leading to management's decisions. For example, consider the "publish or perish" dictum at work in most universities, where faculty must regularly publish in refereed journals to receive merit raises or promotions. Many faculty who excel at this activity are not equally effective in teaching, what many people consider the faculty's primary responsibility. Placing publications ahead of the student's education may arise from the wrong set of values, but as long as the university's administration is constantly beset by funding problems, it must favor the activity that brings in grant money and the kind of recognition that attracts alumni loyalty and donations. Complaining about the university's poor values did nothing for my career and only made me seem naive.

In the ideal world, all managers would have superior analytical and communication skills and take the time to impart these skills to their employees. But, by definition, the ideal is not real, so at one or more points in your career, you will work for a manager who has a communication problem. When you find yourself in this position, you must determine how important this limitation is. If the company is making sound decisions and the manager is relatively competent in organizing the work groups to perform successfully, then it may prove tolerable. (Moreover, in changing groups, you may exchange one problem for another.) However, if you determine the root of your manager's communication problem is insecurity, an unhealthy desire to achieve personally at others' expense, or—as far as you can tell—ignorance or incompetence, you have two ways to improve your situation. You can go to war with the manager, or you can move on. Chapter 4 will focus on recognizing when and how to go to war as well as when you should probably just move on.

## Tips if You Are the Manager

As discussed in chapter 7, most people fantasize about being a great leader followed by an adoring crowd. In actuality, most groups of people in today's culture are hard to interest, much less lead. Consequently, for the manager, particularly the new manager, the following are a number of valuable principles to remember:

- Cynicism is a formidable enemy.

- Email and voice mail are no way to manage.

- Don't confuse confrontation with a lack of commitment.

- Be wary of anyone representing "the People."

- People want things to make sense.

- It is common to fear success as much as failure.

- Everyone aspires to be respected.

- Thinking people anticipate disagreement.

### Cynicism Is a Formidable Enemy

Gossiping and judging others are basic parts of human nature, but in the United States today, a pernicious cynicism has made these tendencies the default mode of response. Some have attributed this behavior to the influence of the media, the electronic age, and our current fixation on enforcing an Ozzie and Harriet lifestyle on a nation whose very foundation was based on freedom of choice. At any rate, the media's addiction to a cycle of adulation, suspicion, and vilification ad nauseum—for example, the interminable O. J. Simpson trial or the Monica Lewinsky saga—regularly reinforces the theme Never trust anyone in power—they're all corrupt, stupid, inferior. This theme is popular not only because it resonates with our innate tendency to judge, but because it gives people an excuse for not holding themselves to a higher standard. They might ask, "If so-and-so is corrupt in light of all his success and perks, then what's the point? How could we ever succeed?"

This attitude—"If management is inept, why should I break my neck around here?"—is deadly in the workplace, because it gives people an excuse for failing. Success in business is hard and getting harder. As a result, every employee, out of self-interest, should be committed to the company's goals, an emotional position that is diametrically opposed to cynicism. Therefore, if you are a manager and have one or more cynics in your group, you should not ignore them but confront them, or you run the risk that they may adversely affect the morale and commitment of your team. To do this effectively, you yourself must be convinced that the company is headed on a *reasonable* course of action. (Note: I do not say the *best* course of action, because every decision in business, much like decisions in personal life, involves certain trade-offs. If after serious efforts to understand the issues you do not believe that your company is following a reasonable course of action, you might want to consider this fight a losing battle and move on.)

Once you are personally armed with the company's rationale, you should confront the cynics you manage, at first privately and then with others, to call their behavior into question. This confrontation does not have to be antagonistic, unless you don't care if the individuals involved leave. In the initial meeting, you can simply say, "You seem to have a problem with the new delivery date/marketing position/whatever. What are you worried about?" Once you have elicited the cynics' specific concerns, you are in a position to address them one by one, with the goal of minimizing them. Even if this tack is successful and the individuals turn into Pollyannas (not likely), you must air this matter publicly at your next group meeting. You don't have to name names. You can just say, "I understand that some of you may be concerned about. . . ." The important thing is to continue to publicly counter negative attitudes until the cynics change their attitude, keep their opinions to themselves, or ultimately decide to leave.

### Email and Voice Mail Are No Way to Manage

Email and voice mail are wonderful tools and can greatly improve productivity, but they are no substitute for face-to-face contact. One of a manager's most important jobs is to motivate employees. To ascertain whether you are successful, you must know and be able to read your employees. While cynics are vocal and love to mouth off, for various reasons many employees are hesitant even to ask questions. They may be afraid that they might seem uncooperative or that they might appear stupid in front of their colleagues. Others are simply shy. One of your challenges is to get quiet and cooperative employees to share their concerns. This kind of communication requires trust, and trust requires that you build a relationship with as many of your direct reports (employees who answer to you) and their direct reports as possible, and you do that through personal contact. Otherwise, you run two risks if the employee becomes discouraged or dissatisfied. He or she will either work less enthusiastically or, worse still, leave.

On a number of occasions, ETI has lost excellent contributors who quit rather than discuss what was concerning them. While an increase in salary was usually involved, money was rarely their major motivator; rather these individuals left hoping that the new company would somehow be different. (And it is, for a while, until he or she becomes dissatisfied with something else and won't speak up.)

## Be Wary of Anyone Representing "the People"

ETI has gone through a number of troubled periods. One of the worst for me personally was when an early manager in development used her influence with the development team to force me into a particular course of action. Because I had been preoccupied with funding and sales, I was slow to realize that this individual had spent a significant amount of energy painting me as a bête noire. Once I realized what was going on—that the company's potential was being held hostage to keep this particular individual satisfied—I fired her. What I didn't anticipate was how effective she had been. One of the team's most valuable technical contributors actually led a campaign to persuade the Board to unseat me. When these efforts failed, other developers began to leave, and some of the people were outstanding. The company meetings during this period—we had about forty people at corporate, then—were pretty stressful. At the low point, after we had lost a few key contributors, two employees asked hard questions at a company meeting. In fact, one of them often prefaced his questions with "I'm probably going to get fired for this, but what about. . . ?" I answered their questions as frankly as I could, and it helped. Their willingness to confront me with their doubts was a sign of their commitment to the company rather than an assault on me, and I appreciated their courage.

One of these people is still with the company; the other joined NASA, with the hope of becoming an astronaut, but still keeps in touch. The one who remains is one of our key technical contributors and continues to ask hard questions. This forthrightness has been a gift because he voices what many people worry about, and his courage helps me understand what people need to know to feel comfortable. In both cases, their directness and my response helped make the other employees feel more comfortable that I wasn't the maniac they had heard about.

## Question the Motive of Someone Representing the People's Voice

Not all leaders are managers. Some individual contributors who may want to manage but don't feel comfortable with all the requirements are nevertheless emotional leaders. They are respected for the value of their own work and for their concern for others and their success. These people can be invaluable to the organization, in part because their leadership does not include the trappings of power associated with management. An emotional leader whose motives are pure will rarely pose as a spokesperson. Rather they will work to try to help fellow employees feel better on an individual basis. As a manager, it is important to recognize this kind of emotional leader, because if you can give him a vision he can believe in, he can make a tremendous difference in morale.

Occasionally, however, you will encounter an emotional leader whose goal is to foster individual power rather than promote the good of the company. Sometimes they try to lead a palace revolt, as discussed in the previous section; other times they simply seek self-validation. The latter instance is less dramatic but in many ways every bit as destructive. As an example, consider M, a reasonably talented technical individual ETI hired for a particular project in the days before we had strong management in development. He was a solid performer in terms of his commitment and effort but not the quality of his work. As we began to implement sophisticated project management within the organization and he was placed under closer scrutiny and more pressure (incidentally at about the same time he was going through a divorce), he began to position himself as the confidante of all the developers in his area. As he heard their concerns, rather than encouraging them to voice them directly to management, which would have helped build company solidarity, he would nod, say that he understood, and agree with their concern. Later, at a key meeting where the VP in charge of development was making an unpopular announcement—he was not going to recommend quarterly bonuses for the group members because they had not met their goals—M stated that he spoke for all the developers in that group and that if the VP did not reconsider that recommendation he could count on a mass walkout. The VP capitulated but strongly stated he would not make such a concession again.

Ignoring the outcome of the particular decision, consider what M did in terms of a warfare scenario: He held his manager hostage at the expense of the company. If the VP had been a leader on a battlefield, he could have shot M on the spot and ruled by fear. In business, dealing with a spokesperson is not so simple. On the one hand, if the company immediately punishes the spokesperson, other employees get the message that it is dangerous to speak their minds. On the other hand, left unchecked, this sort of individual often uses his influence with his colleagues to work against your goals as a manager.

As a manager, it is critical then that you stop this spokesperson's behavior. The best way to remove the individual's chance to serve as the voice of the people is by dealing with them directly yourself. This process takes time and skill, because it does no good to talk to individual employees if you don't also comfort and motivate them. Then, as the employees begin to trust you, the power of the spokesperson diminishes and the individual gets what he or she deserves because, in general, people who assume this role do so because they would rather gossip than work. In the meantime, while becoming more involved with the individual employees, you may well discover someone who could be an effective leader and serve as a constructive spokesperson for the people who work for or with him.

## People Want Things to Make Sense

We have discussed types of communication that can signal a serious problem to you if you are a manager. Now let's focus on how you can motivate the people who work for you. Even the least intellectually curious or aggressive people still want to think that what they are being asked to do at work makes sense and that, on a larger scale, what the company as a whole is doing makes sense. Therefore, ask yourself what you believe your employees know about the company's direction and the pressures it is under. Then you need to explain why their projects are important in the context of the company's current position and goals. I have found that the biggest single failing in managers (including myself) is not giving employees enough information. Either they assume that the employees know everything the managers know, or they don't believe the employees need to know or are interested. In either case, this failure to share information can be one of the biggest unnecessary causes of morale problems. Just remember, people want their jobs to make sense.

## It Is Common to Fear Success as Much as Failure

It's safe to say that no one wants to sincerely attempt something and fail. When someone else signs employees up for the battle, as is often the case with management, they are even more insecure. Consequently, as you try to motivate your employees, it is important to acknowledge their concerns (for example, they may know nothing about a particular operating system or piece of hardware) while encouraging them to commit to success in spite of these uncertainties. Too often when facing a hard technical problem, programmers have told me that they couldn't guarantee completing a project by a particular date. I can't tell you how many times I've responded by saying, "Well, I know one way to guarantee that we won't succeed, and that's if we don't even try." Even with the most dedicated teams, people commonly fall short of meeting the ultimate goal. To push people to achieve their best, though, their goal usually has to be high, and they have to face a risk of not making it.

Managers must also recognize that people are often uncomfortable with success and, after the high fives and champagne, that some have nagging fears that they could have just as easily failed or that their success was somehow dependent upon luck. If you have an employee who strongly feels that way, he or she may be unwilling to take on such new challenges as becoming a team leader or manager. You may fail to encourage those employees who are not buoyed by their past successes, but one way you can reduce their fear of facing risk is by letting them off the hook when they make a mistake or try a new type of project and do not succeed.

Then there are your natural warriors, or employees who cannot do anything but take on the battle and the challenge. If they are talented and succeed most of the time, they become severely disappointed in themselves when they do fail. In these cases, I have found it useful to compare them to racehorses. A good racehorse loves to run, loves to win, and runs its best in every race. But a good trainer knows that for the horse's health and continued success, it needs to stay out of races periodically to rebuild its strength. As with a racehorse, try to help the warrior learn to pace herself, because in business, we are always at war and at risk. If putting all of her energies into a single battle or even the next three battles could decide the outcome, then it might be worth it for the employee to give every project heroic efforts. But in business she will always face another battle, and if your natural warrior doesn't learn to recognize fatigue and pace herself, she will ultimately either become discouraged and less productive or quit, hoping that the next job will prove different (which, of course it rarely is).

## Everyone Aspires to Be Respected

As we will discuss in chapter 8, at some level most people want to respect people in power and authority and be judged fairly but favorably. This desire, however, is about as realistic as the ideal parent. While some managers—and parents—approach the ideal, all people have their shortcomings. As a result, it is likely that some of the people you manage do not respect you. However, any manager can benefit from remembering one thing: Everyone wants to be respected. The best way to approach employees then is with respect, assuming that they are professional and would wish the best for the company. This effort becomes more difficult when you have observed negative behavior in an employee, and I can honestly say that I have not always followed this advice.

This tactic, however, did serve me well in one very negative situation. I struggled with a senior manager I had hired at an exorbitant salary and bonus plan to rebuild an organization that was critical to the company's success. C had a great track record, but a different style and approach. C had also wanted his next position to be that of CEO, or at the very least COO (chief operating officer in charge of managing everything but investor relations). I told him that if he succeeded in his initial charter, he might well be a good candidate for the job.

C accepted the offer, but within months after he joined the company I worried that I had made a serious mistake. It was not just our differences in style; he didn't want to have anything to do with me. I had always spent time with senior managers immediately after they were hired to discuss their impressions of the product and employees and to build our mutual trust but C considered this model micromanaging. I tried every trick in my book to align us, but nothing worked. The rest of my management team, who had the same doubts I did, was disgusted. While he began to rebuild the most critical part of his organization, he gave little or no attention to the other people he managed.

I thought C was putting the company at unnecessary risk. I didn't want to go to war with him, however, because the company had already suffered a serious setback from the failure of the organization in question and to become openly hostile to the very person I had brought in to fix the problem would have been deadly for morale. At the time a good friend of mine who was a martial artist continually coached me to visualize myself as a great leader and not let C get to me. He said, "You have the authority, he works for you. Tell him what you want as if you expect to get it, but always remember, `respect brings respect.'" I followed that advice, showing no irritation but being persistent in asking C for what I wanted. C became quite frustrated that I kept "micromanaging" him but could do little but comply, because I was so calm and respectful.

Shortly before the Board meeting, I had breakfast with Bob Inman. In outlining what I felt good about and what I was worried about, I mentioned that I was concerned that some of C's behavior appeared destructive to the company, for example, his telling everyone that we should sell the company, his tendency to complain about my decisions to everyone but me, and his relationship with a female employee. I ended by saying that I believed it was in the company's best interest for me to downplay our differences and manage around him, but I wanted Bob to be aware of the problem.

About five weeks after the Board meeting, I asked C for a status report, and at the end of it, he told me he was leaving the company. At first I was extremely upset as I thought his departure would send a terrible signal to the employees, the Board and the marketplace. I told C to give it a week, that I might be willing to "buy" his time to stay on a bit longer. However, after consultation with the Board, I concluded that his behavior with the employees and various Board members had been targeted at undermining me.

I had benefited from taking the high road and treating him with respect, because it was then clear that C had had the political agenda and not me. If I had been at war with him, the issues might have been clouded. It might have appeared as if I had been threatened by C, in which case the correct path for the company would have been less certain. In short, street fights are to be avoided and you rarely lose by treating someone with respect.

### Thinking People Anticipate Disagreement

Finally, in strategizing how to motivate the employees who report to you, it is important to anticipate which of them might disagree with the company's assumptions and for what reason. It is always more effective for you to deal with these concerns before they have to ask, suggesting that you (and the company) have fully thought the matter through. If an employee raises the objection first, it leaves the suggestion that there may be other equally reasonable objections that you have not yet considered.

Moreover, when answering the objection, avoid diminishing the objector's concerns or values, and argue that while her points are valid, there are good reasons for their reduced priority in the short term. For example, if you tell someone specializing in user interface that improving the product's interface is not important, they will focus on why you are either stupid or wrong. Instead you might say, for example, that you too believe that it is critical for the company to invest in improving the interface, but the cost of supporting the product's database layer is significantly reducing the profit margin so the company feels that it has to give that work priority.

## What You Can Learn from Observing Others

### Communication between Peers

We have been focusing on communication between people with different levels of authority in the company. However, it is equally important to accurately assess your colleagues to determine their level of credibility and to understand how to enlist their support. This task is both simplified and complicated by the fact that you are likely to see these individuals in a broader variety of situations. For example, even in the most democratic of companies of any size, it is unlikely that senior management will spend much time chatting with employees in the coffee room, not because they don't believe that such dialogues would be informative or enjoyable, but because they frequently don't have the time to socialize and get their jobs done. Chatting informally about topics other than work, for example, hobbies or children, gives you a better sense of what a person is really like. And yet this increased intimacy, and the desire to maintain it, can complicate your ability to act in the company's best interest.

For example, when a relationship is purely professional between peers, employees usually feel an obligation to voice their agreement or disagreement when a colleague makes a judgment about the workplace. However, we all want more latitude in our personal relationships, or the right to voice what we feel without having to argue authoritatively that our opinion is correct. As a result, many people are uncomfortable about disagreeing with someone with whom they have been talking about personal as well as professional matters. This situation can sometimes result in their feeling like they are in a double bind. On a number of occasions I have learned too late from employees that someone felt unfairly treated by his manager or bored in his current position when, if management had known about the situation, the manager could have remedied it. When I indicated that I wished they had told me about the other person's dissatisfaction, these employees replied that they were afraid that they might have betrayed a confidence if they had alerted anyone in management. They also indicated that they weren't comfortable disagreeing with or encouraging the person to come forward on his or her own. No one wins in these situations, not management, the unhappy employee, or the confidante who feels that they have done no one a service.

## Common Personality Types

Despite these complications, there are a number of reasons that it is valuable to become adept at reading your colleagues' patterns of communication and what they may imply about their character. These people may become members of your team, and you may depend on them for your own personal success. You may become their manager. Or you may at some point go to war in the organization and benefit from understanding how they, either wittingly or unwittingly, can be used as allies or weapons. In any case, when analyzing colleagues, it is important to contrast their public and private behavior. If it is inconsistent, you should make an effort to determine what this inconsistency means. Sometimes people have different styles or different levels of candor depending upon the setting. They may be jovial and outspoken when they're with friends but very shy in front of people who have authority over them. This behavior is not particularly damning in and of itself, as many people feel insecure or self-conscious around people in authority. However, if when among peers the individual in question always holds forth about how the company's screwing up or what the company ought to do and then is silent around management, you probably shouldn't rely on them if you go to war. Odds are they can't be counted on.

In short, you can often deduce a great deal about a person by observing how they communicate. I have compiled a list of different personality types that is by no means exhaustive, but it will illustrate the point. People may evolve from one of these modes to another over time as they develop, or fail to develop, emotionally. You can use these stereotypes to develop your own classification system and warning signals regarding whom and what to trust.

*The Cynic.* There are two types of cynic—one has a pet peeve but is otherwise basically positive on other topics while the other, the chronic cynic, frequently expresses distrust or disbelief. With the chronic cynic there is always an undercurrent of commentary, more or less publicly expressed. You'll hear the chronic cynic using phrases like "as if the sales team knows anything about what the customer wants" or "H won't fight with T about the unreasonable schedules because he's kissing up for a promotion." As indicated earlier in the chapter, this cynic can be a negative force on a team. You will find that chronic cynics almost never directly confront problems in a context where he or she could actually make a difference because that would rob them of their favorite pastime of criticizing others. And why is this behavior so important to them? At the risk of overgeneralizing, I believe that at some level it gives them an excuse for being less than committed. Trust 'em in a pinch? Better not.

***The Complainer.*** Although they are both characterized by a negative attitude, a complainer is not necessarily a cynic. A cynic always assumes the worst about the person or organization in question—for example, the person is stupid or the organization is hopelessly corrupt—while a complainer is less concerned about naming the evil in others than in thinking that life is too hard or the world is not fair. H is a friend of mine whom I met through work and who was good to me during a difficult period of my life. One of the reasons that H and I bonded is that we both had a history of low self-esteem, which we have spent most of our adult lives growing out of. Both of us are significantly better off than we were ten years ago, although my professional life has been more lucrative. (Hers has been more flexible, however, with respect to time.) As H became more secure and began to feel more deserving, she became less self-deprecating and better able to assert herself professionally. However, a good part of what still holds H back is that she thinks the world isn't fair. She once told me that it didn't bother her that I was successful, but it upset her that so many of her acquaintances, who were less talented or deserving than she, had become successful.

Most of us feel the need to complain from time to time. In fact, one of the benefits of marriage is having someone with a vested interest in your well-being whom you can complain to. But if complaining constitutes too much of what someone conveys, they are probably not someone that you want to depend on. They perform professionally, but their worldview gives them an excuse for failure.

**The Worrier.** You might confuse a worrier with a complainer since both of them tend to focus on the negative. The major difference is that worriers focus less on whether something is fair or someone is deserving and more on factors that affect their ability to succeed. One of our most talented members of the technical staff is a worrier. When presented with a business need to deliver a solution within a particular timeframe, F's face will darken, he'll begin to chew on what can go wrong, and only when he's reasonably sure that most of the "gotchas" have been identified and some plan is in place for tracking them will he begin to relax. As a result, F is an extremely valuable member of any time-critical team, because even though his initial hesitance to buy into a schedule is sometimes annoying, his approach helps ensure that the team encounters a minimum number of surprises. In short, having a worrier who is otherwise loyal and professional on your team can help reduce risk in warfare.

**The Firebrand.** The firebrand is often perceived, and rightly so, as a hothead or revolutionary. Unlike the cynic, who prefers to make such sneak attacks as the sly aside or the cocktail party imitation, the firebrand is hell-bent on making his dissatisfaction known to as broad an audience as possible. While the firebrand demonstrates courage in his willingness to take risks, his lack of judgment makes him a questionable ally. The question to ask when evaluating a firebrand is, What is the target of his anger? In more cases than not, you will find that the firebrand focuses too much on the people responsible for a bad decision and not enough on how to get around these people. In other words, using the terms from the introduction, firebrands tend to see themselves as warriors, focused primarily on defeating anyone they encounter who exhibits the "wrong" value system rather than ignoring the person and focusing on the goal.

From the time I started working at Texas Instruments in 1981 until 1987, when I had experienced significant defeat and humiliation at MCC, I was a firebrand, outraged at any individual employee who shirked his duty (whether a technical writer who failed to incorporate the comments I had so laboriously researched for her or a colleague who spent two or three hours a day creating softball schedules) or at my manager who was stupid enough not to be equally enraged. In looking back on those days that were characterized predominantly by anger, I realize I was too focused on justice and the need to have my values validated. People have different perspectives, strengths, and levels of commitment; organizations are inefficient; and life is not fair; but at some level, I felt that expressing my rage—loud enough and to enough people—would somehow make a difference. What it mostly did was make other people uncomfortable with and alienated from me. It took years of suffering from the same mistakes and working with a therapist for me to tease out how much of my rage was rooted in childhood fears and how much arose from my low self-esteem before I was able to make the transition to an adventurer.

***The Victim.*** Like the firebrand, the victim is driven by an obsession that the world is not fair, but the focus is different. While they both may focus on identifying who is evil and what is unfair, the firebrand wants to change the world. The victim, on the other hand, feels somehow vindicated because the lack of fairness explains why they are not more successful and why they deserve sympathy. The victim then is far less disruptive than the firebrand but nevertheless still destructive. The firebrand's unrelenting rage usually alienates coworkers. The victim, on the other hand, can often find a sympathetic audience, and the time they take from their coworkers and any concern they engender regarding the company's leadership have negative effects on the team's morale and performance. Since victims are looking for an excuse for failure, they can never be counted on for anything but a willingness to commiserate.

Note that many of these communicative postures are rooted in spiritual and emotional limitations that can only be changed by the personal commitment of the person exhibiting them. As a manager, I once tried to help a victim break through her negative attitudes by promoting her to a team leadership position. I thought that her promotion would validate her self-worth and that it would motivate her to stop focusing on the limitations of the others in the organization. (Wrong.) Rather than rising to the occasion, she simply found other things that robbed her of chances at the success that was due her. Observing this behavior, I tried being direct, saying that as long as she saw herself as an unloved child, she was destined to be one. (Even worse.) If someone is expending an enormous amount of energy to avoid facing some fear, she is not going to appreciate you exposing that fear. In fact, the employee in question left shortly after this conversation and has never forgiven me, from what I hear, for being such an ogre.

***The Networker.*** Compared to many types we have discussed above, the networker is relatively benign. Rather than focusing on others' failures or limitations, the networker is more concerned with helping build others' reputations and your knowledge of his relationship with these important folks. The goal of the networker, of course, is to make you want to be connected with him. Many of these individuals actually do accomplish, in part through their networking, a great deal of good. Other networkers don't only focus on who they know but also on what they know, what they've done, and what they have. Maybe it's the fact that she knows about travel or wine or her car, but this networker's goal is to establish her power. This attitude is not bad in and of itself, but the more you notice that networker's focus is on establishing her power instead of on the nuts and bolts of the tasks that must be accomplished to succeed, the less you should be impressed by her value as an ally.

*The Armchair Quarterback.* Given that this posture is one of the most popular sports in the United States, I guess I should go easy here. The armchair quarterback likes to make the calls that he believes the quarterback on the football field should have made. As long as these opinions are not cynical or judgmental, this propensity is not particularly damaging unless the individual in question is one of the designated leaders of a group or company. In this case, the individual owes his opinions to the company and not to the audience sitting to his right at the table. If you see a manager exhibit this behavior, you must assume that the individual in question lacks courage or else he would voice his opinions to his boss. This individual may fulfill his particular duties with some level of professionalism, but the organization will not get the benefit of his ideas.

*The Smooth Operator.* The smooth operator is frequently an extremely effective employee or manager because everything he does is geared at optimizing his ability to succeed in business. The operator's goal is to maximize his support throughout the organization while minimizing his risk. He is affable and personable and rarely directly confronts or criticizes anyone. He has valuable opinions and insights, but he offers only enough information to win credibility without giving away anything that can be used to his advantage elsewhere. He works to succeed within the power structure, and so to him information is power. His efforts at building relationships are intended to make the majority of people comfortable with him in case he is promoted. A smooth operator can be a valuable ally if you are in a position to reward him and he does not perceive your efforts as revolutionary. Because his goal is to win power within the existing organization, the smooth operator cannot be trusted if your battle puts you at risk in the organization.

**The Confessor.** Certain individuals invite the trust and confidences of others because of their warmth and sincerity. However, unlike in church, the confessions they hear are less a matter of soul-searching than of their colleagues' fears and feelings. They focus on others' opinions, such as the boss is insensitive, we'll never make the delivery date promised, or the consultants are doing a terrible job. Confessors convince themselves that they are doing the organization a service, and without their understanding ear, employee X might quit. The problem is that the confessor doesn't use the information he learns to improve anything; rather he hoards these confidences like they were gold because they make him feel important and give him his power. Even if he chooses to be a spokesperson, to put himself forth as the representative of those who confide in him, he rarely will be sufficiently direct about the problems people are having to allow others to help solve them. Whether you're a manager looking for a leader in your group or for that quality in a colleague, don't count on the confessor.

**The Healer.** The healer has many of the same skills as the confessor, and her colleagues trust and confide in her. Unlike the confessor, the healer takes no comfort in other people's distress and tries to find ways to help the individual confiding in her. Sometimes she's merely providing the individual with assurances. Sometimes the healer, without revealing her source, will bring the problem in question to management's attention; consequently, the individual who confided in her benefits from having his problem solved and finds the healer more trustworthy. Obviously, the difference between the healer and the confessor is the very reason that the healer is someone you can trust, as long as your motives and goals are directed toward the general good: Unlike the confessor, the healer finds satisfaction in harmony and teamwork.

**The Silent.** Many people are not comfortable sharing their feelings at work. Sometimes it's because they are shy about expressing their feelings in general. In other cases, they may believe that they owe the company their loyalty without question, much like dutiful soldiers. In still others, the individual is a cynic or just lazy and doesn't want to get caught. Some silent types are not totally silent. They will talk about movies, the weather, or any general topic, but they avoid talking about substantive or controversial work-related issues.

How you assess whether to trust a silent type then must be based on something besides words. If they exhibit a professionalism and pride in their work and are appreciative and supportive of their colleagues, they are clearly assets that the company should value and the kind of person you would want to understand your position and support you should you go to battle within your organization. You should not try to obtain their commitment in a public forum, as they will immediately react negatively to being put on the spot. Instead have a tête-à-tête with each of them to ask what they think about your position.

Another important thing to remember about silent types, whether you are their manager or colleague, is that you may miss the fact when they become discouraged or disheartened since frequently their body language is also not expressive. On more than one occasion the company has lost highly valued employees because by the time management became aware that they were unhappy, they were already committed to go elsewhere. Consequently, if you have classified someone as a silent type and you want to keep that employee working for you, you should make an effort to build a one-on-one relationship with him. Even if he never confides directly to you, he will feel valued, which should make it harder for him to leave without talking to you first.

## Developing Your Own Voice Professionally and Personally

We have spent much of this chapter discussing what can be deduced from observing how other people communicate. You should also become aware of how you communicate, what your style conveys to others, and, most important, what it tells you about your fears and anger. Much of our behavior is instinctive, and often the immediate feeling is a mask for the real emotion. Many years ago a friend told me about a book he read called something like *Self Therapy*. The insight I remember from our discussion was the author's claim that whenever you have an excessively strong emotion, it is usually masking another even stronger emotion that you are afraid to face. For example, if a parent walked into an upstairs bedroom and saw a toddler about to fall out the window, he or she would be likely to grab and scold the child, apparently full of anger when the real emotion was fear.

In my own case, when I finally acknowledged on an emotional level that my well-being and that of my daughters was my sole responsibility, I moved my family to Austin and went to work for Texas Instruments. There, anyone who failed to perform in what I considered the company's best interest, including my boss, filled me with rage. At home I bitterly complained about them, causing my heart and my breathing rate to increase. My eyes would narrow, and my lips tighten whenever I thought about them. I went to bed angry and woke up angry. Although I was so consumed by my feelings, I never stopped to ask myself why I was so focused on my boss's failings, and I didn't spend some of that energy figuring out how to get the company to succeed in spite of him. Several years and another "bad boss" later, I looked beneath the mask and began to separate my anger at work from my fear of my inability to take care of myself and my kids.

Neurolinguists maintain that often you can change your perception of your emotional well-being by changing your linguistic habits. By becoming aware of what you are focusing on in your interactions with others, you can determine what your fears are and, with work, overcome them. If words are your weapons, then you must master them. This initiative requires a cycle of analysis, insight, and conscious effort to change behavior that isn't serving you.

Just as a soldier trains to fight in different types of terrain, you should sharpen your skills so that you can be effective in a large variety of situations, written and oral. As you become more self-aware of how and what you are communicating, you will improve your ability to deal with various types of conflict effectively. In the coming chapters, we will examine what skills are required to support each type of engagement.

# Chapter 4

# Modes of Battle
## Strategies for Dealing with Conflict

S oldiers train to achieve mastery of weapons, to build endurance, and to hone their ability to assess and address risk. Most of us become soldiers reluctantly. Whether some innate fear or social imperative makes us feel uncomfortable with conflict, I have always been amazed—even when I myself was equally terrified of going to war—at how much pain most of us will endure over long periods rather than take the risk and face someone's anger by taking up arms. In this chapter we will examine the relationship between fear and anger and how fear, if unaddressed, either becomes self-fulfilling or stultifying. Once we have focused on how fear manifests itself in the workplace, we will characterize different types of conflict and the mode of warfare best suited to addressing each.

## The Internal Battle: Fear and Anger

Heroic literature frequently focuses on the hero's ability to act in spite of fear. In the first chapter of *Dune*[1]—the first book in Frank Herbert's classic science fiction trilogy—Reverend Mother tests the young hero, Paul, by asking him to place his hand in a box and endure whatever pain he encounters. At this point Paul recalls the response from the Litany of Fear, which, as his mother taught him from the Bene Gesserit rite, states, "Fear is the mindkiller." In the great Scandinavian epic, the *Volsunga Saga*,[2] Sigmund is tasked by his twin sister, Signy, to train one of her three sons to avenge the death of their father and brothers at the hands of her husband. She sends her first son to Sigmund, who lives in the forest. Before suppertime, Sigmund tells his nephew to bake bread while Sigmund chops wood. When he returns and discovers the boy has refused to bake because something was moving in the bag of flour, Sigmund kills him, saying, "You're not worthy to be a Volsung." Signy's second son encounters a similar fate. Signy's youngest son, Sinfjotli, baked the bread, after killing a serpent his uncle had left in the flour bag. Sigmund then declared the brave boy was worthy to be a Volsung, and years later they successfully avenged the wrong to their family.

The difference between a hero and the general populace then is not the benefits of birth or superior skills, but his relationship to fear. A hero is not fearless. What would be heroic in that? Rather a hero finds the courage to face his fears and, for some time at least, the skill to defeat them. While many of us do not face physical danger in the workplace, most of us experience fear. Sometimes the fear is as simple and direct as being afraid that we do not have the skills to successfully perform some assigned task or that we have made some mistake for which we will be judged badly. However, other times our fear is less easy to recognize, and that is usually when it takes the form of anger or indignation. Let's explore some theories about how humans learn and respond and how our reactions can often adversely affect our ability to understand what we really feel.

For years psychologists have argued that the process of learning is a matter of using sensory perceptions to discriminate. The behaviorists believed that this process of discrimination involved learning to generalize. In other words, every face or chair was initially perceived as unique and distinct entities, and development was the ability to recognize similarities. In the mid-1970s, experimental psychologists' work suggested the opposite: The infant's innate perception was essentially relative; learning was based on the ability to differentiate or recognize absolute differences. But whether the learning process is essentially inductive or deductive—or a combination of both—the point is that perception and understanding are active rather than reactive processes. This fact has been further verified in psycholinguistic experiments that suggest that what people perceive when they read or hear is in good part a function of what they predict they will read or hear. In reading studies, researchers asked bilingual subjects to read for content under time pressure and found that they could freely intermix the two languages in the text without the subjects ever having noticed. Similarly, researchers studying the perception of spoken language originally assumed that some set of acoustic invariants in each sound in a language would account for our recognizing an $a$ from an $o$ and a $p$ from a $b$. Spectographic analysis found no evidence of these invariants, however, leading researchers to believe that speech perception is significantly more active than previously thought. People hear a $p$ instead of a $b$ because that sound is what they expect to hear given the context of what is being said.[3] The fact that we as animals can perform such tasks with little or no conscious effort is surely a miracle and that humans can imagine and execute elaborate plans is even more so. However, perhaps because these skills are so innate and effective we often fail to develop the self-awareness to question our perceptions. For our own personal growth, it is critical that we do analyze them, particularly when strong emotions are involved.

Modern psychology has many theories regarding the various aspects of the personality, but one of the most helpful set of distinctions I have encountered is outlined in Serge King's book *Mastering Your Hidden Self—A Guide to the Huna Way*.[4] A psychologist, King attempts to explain the concepts found in the Huna philosophy, which originated in ancient times in Polynesia. Although Huna recognizes seven aspects that make up each individual, most important to our discussion are the three that characterize the mind:

■ *The* ku, *or subconscious.* Analogous to Freud's id, the ku differs in that it does not constitute the wild and unruly aspects of the individual that must be controlled by the ego and reconciled with the superego. In Huna philosophy, the ku controls most of the bodily and some of the mental functions. It is the first feature of the mind to develop and has the following functions and attributes.

1. Its primary purpose is memory.

2. It controls the entire operation of the physical body, though some of the control is shared by the conscious mind *(lono).*

3. It is the source of all emotions and feelings.

4. It is the receiver and transmitter of all psychic phenomena.

5. Its prime directive is to grow.

6. It reasons logically.

7. It obeys orders.[5]

■ *The* lono, *or conscious.* The lono develops later than the ku, and its primary attribute is will power, or the ability to direct one's awareness and intention in response to a thought or experience.

■ *The* aumakua, *or superconscious.* This aspect of the mind is the "God within" that gives guidance, information, and inspiration but never orders.

The unconscious is an obedient and rational servant that is usually efficient in prioritizing what we need to pay attention to and what we can ignore. King maintains that the unconscious is so efficient that sometimes the conscious mind accepts its analysis without question. However, since the unconscious mind develops earlier than the conscious, sometimes the conclusions it draws are wrong. If a child's parent has a violent temper, for example, the unconscious might quite correctly assess that a raised voice should inspire fear. The problem is that, thirty years later, it may cause the body to respond with the same urgency, leading the individual to respond with greater intensity than the situation warrants. An individual who encounters this kind of event frequently but fails to learn to discount the intensity of his reaction runs the risk of either suffering more anxiety than necessary or reacting inappropriately to situations.

The message here is not to disregard intense reactions, attributing them to early imprinting while a child. You need to acknowledge that the intensity of your reaction is usually tied to the level of risk you believe that you are encountering. For example, in the case of the individual with a violent parent, all raised voices may cause alarm, but the intensity may be tied to how vulnerable the person feels. For example, hearing your brother-in-law yell may be extremely upsetting, but odds are you will feel the emotion even more strongly if the person yelling is your husband or manager. The point is to apply conscious analysis to determining how much the intensity of your reaction is tied to the external situation. If you emotionally give an enemy more power than he deserves, you probably will not choose the kind of warfare best suited to defeat him. Remember, the body never lies; it just doesn't speak in English. In developing your skills as a warrior, it is always important to understand how much of the battle should be waged with the enemy and how much with yourself.

It is not important that you adopt the Huna characterization of the mind. I have used a number of other metaphors. What is important is that you must learn to step back from any intense negative emotion you feel and try to understand if the situation inciting these feelings warrants that level of response. If not, then you must work as hard to recognize and defeat your internal enemy as you do in fighting the external battle. Moreover, the internal enemy in all of us, like Loki, is a trickster and may wear many masks, appearing repeatedly in various situations at different points in our lives, making him hard to recognize as one and the same.[6] But as you learn to outwit him in each of these masks and get closer to his core, you will find that his name is fear, and as you get closer to his essence, the more likely the fear will be something rooted in your early, sometimes preverbal, past.

## The External Battle: Types of Warfare

We spent the first part of this chapter focusing on how to recognize when an intense reaction to a situation is due to a resonance between your inner enemy and the enemy you face in the external world. In the rest of this chapter we will examine several common types of conflict and the best strategies for taking on each type of warfare. Some of these battles—like "gaining a commission," when you have the right goal and the right support—are rather benign. Others, as in the case when you are faced with a hostile and unjust assault from without, are much more dangerous and threatening. In each case, we will consider the defining characteristics as well as the typical degree of risk involved to help you determine whether you are willing to take on the cost of the engagement.

### Gaining a Commission

Some psychologists have argued that one of the most damning assumptions of modern psychology is that a healthy personality is a consistent personality when, in fact, most of us have many different aspects that are not consistent. Instead, good mental health might consist of finding a means where most of those facets of one's personality have an opportunity to contribute to the individual's life. One could argue that, in part, this pursuit is what makes having a fulfilling marriage hard. To operate efficiently in the relationship, we learn to characterize what our partner likes or dislikes and to interact with that person accordingly. As a result, over the years a mate frequently finds it difficult to express or be recognized for anything that doesn't fit the mold. If a partner fails to recognize too many aspects of the other, then the marriage often fails.

Companies are no different. As they grow, they develop procedures and organizations that made sense at one time but may actually work against the company's success later. For example, when I worked at TI, organizations were managed along functional lines. A pool of people designed and wrote the software, another tested it, another documented it, another developed training, and so on. While having a pool of resources with common processes and procedures for each function at some level made sense, in actuality it was extremely inefficient. The problem was people from each group were arbitrarily assigned to a product cycle for a particular period, and if the schedule slipped, you would lose that resource and be assigned someone new. In my case, I was on a three-person (programmer) project for a new release of a product. Halfway through the project, the project manager quit, and then three weeks before the product went into system test, the second senior person quit. In both cases we had to postpone the product delivery date, and we lost the individuals assigned from test and technical publications. Consequently, the technical team (which finally consisted of one person—me) had to train two sets of two people on the same information before they could do their jobs. The result was further delays and a lower-quality product.

Next I was assigned to an extremely visible project where

we had to adapt a research laboratory prototype of a natural language interface subsystem to the initial release of the TI PC. My team was told the company had to be able to demonstrate the prototype at a trade show in December and the product delivery would take place in May. Our task was complicated because none of the six programmers assigned to the project had ever programmed in the designated programming language (C) and the company only bought three IBM PCs for us to work on, telling us that "engineering models" would be available within four weeks. By the end of six weeks, we were still taking turns using the IBM PCs and still on the waiting list for engineering PCs. After my manager simply kept shrugging his shoulders in response to our requests for his intervention, I complained bitterly to my manager's manager. Using the project's visibility and importance, I chose to draw the battle lines and I "gained a commission." Not only did we get our three engineering models within twenty-four hours, but we had a person in test and a person in documentation permanently assigned to the project so that they could become fluent in the product and maximally effective in their tasks. My manager's superior broke the rules, but he succeeded with little consequence partially because he did the right thing and because the team committed and delivered on deadline.

Gaining a commission is possible when:

- The company recognizes the goal's importance. For example, all my caterwauling about how much money we could make selling our software package on the IBM PC as well as the TI PC amounted to nothing in a company where IBM was the "evil empire" and hardware was king. Only delivering on deadline counted.

- Your manager is supportive.

- You are committed to delivering for your manager if he obtains what you say you need.

Remember, however, that gaining a commission is signing up to deliver as a subordinate. It is not important that you be publicly identified as the leader or the hero. Deliver, and you will get the credit. Don't, and you probably won't get a second chance. Note also that delivering doesn't mean hiding problems when you encounter them, but taking responsibility for recognizing and solving them.

## Breaking Ranks

Even under the same business conditions, gaining a commission is not possible when you have a hostile manager. As indicated elsewhere, your manager may be hostile to you for a number of reasons, such as your differences in values, in style, or in attitudes. The reason does not really matter unless something about your manager or your interaction with her triggers your inner enemy. In that case, you are apt to focus as much on the manager as on the problem you are trying to solve for the company and that distraction isn't going to help you or the company, because the odds of your instigating a change in your manager's character or attitudes are pretty slim. (Remember, if it's going to take therapy to fix your manager, leave.)

The problem is many such conflicts evolve so that you may not recognize how much time you are spending worrying about the relationship. That was exactly the case with my first manager in the software industry, B. When I first interviewed with him, I didn't particularly take to B, nor he to me, but I was nervous about changing professions and took his coolness as justifiable doubt about whether I could succeed. During the first six months, I became increasingly frustrated with him because whenever I made a suggestion to improve the process or efficiency, he would reply that it was a good idea but simply couldn't be done.

I then made the mistake of speaking very harshly about the incompetent behavior of the support personnel assigned to our project. In one case, I was angry after I had edited the draft of a manual only to receive the next draft with most of the errors still uncorrected. In another case, I wrote a rough draft of what the test plan should include (approximately thirteen or so pages) and gave it to the person assigned in test to help her get a head start on designing the necessary test databases and programs. Weeks later the individual gave me the final test plan, which consisted of my original document (unchanged) with a cover sheet. I was furious. Here we were, shorthanded on the project, and our time was being wasted. I became so caught up in my sense of what was right that I didn't notice how uncomfortable my anger made my manager.

In retrospect, I now realize that B avoided any form of conflict so he must have found my "in your face" expressions of anger particularly distasteful. An interesting side note—and evidence of his fear of taking risks—was that B was also an "ABD" from a prestigious university, meaning he had completed *all* the requirements for a doctorate *but* the writing and defense of his dissertation. Albeit in a nontechnical field from a less prestigious university, I have a Ph.D, which no doubt irritated him even more. However, at the time I couldn't appreciate B's problems because I was so caught up in my own excessive anger at what "wasn't right." B got the first lick in at my annual review. He gave me a fair to middling raise (after I had worked like a slave) and included the comment "Kay is sometimes her own worst enemy . . ." along with observations about my temperament. This treatment made me even madder, but once again I was not sufficiently dispassionate to look at our interactions objectively. Then I decided to consciously work on my interactions with him and to control my temper. I even invited B and his wife to dinner. Nothing helped. When we worked on the highly visible natural language interface subsystem described above and B's "there's nothing I can do" management approach threatened our ability to deliver by the deadline, I finally broke ranks and went to his boss, M, who gave me a commission.

There are risks associated with breaking ranks, however. If the other manager you approach is hierarchical, he may consider your approach insubordinate. If your values and performance are not yet recognized in the organization, you could be perceived as arrogant or rash. On a number of occasions, relatively new employees have told me that it is critical that we change the way we do this or that. Often their ideas are sound, but the management team has already considered them and has a valid reason for not utilizing them. We may not have the cash or there may be a more pressing priority. Occasionally, however, employees simply don't like their manager's style. In any case, I always ask if they have discussed these issues with their manager. If an employee hedges his answer or says no and I trust the manager (and managers I don't trust don't last long), then I assume that the employee is political and trying to look good at the manager's expense. I typically follow up with the manager in question, in some cases directly and in others without making it clear that the employee has specifically talked to me. If I am certain that the manager is secure, knows I trust him, and can deal with dissension without prejudice, I will come out and say that X scheduled time with me to discuss his concerns. In the latter case, I may just bring up the topic in a regular status session, saying, for example, "I understand that there's some talk that the release may not be stable in time to go to beta." The manager's reaction and recollection of the previous discussions reveal whether the topic has been discussed in the group, whether the trade-offs he has opted for make sense, and so on. If my take on this discussion is that both the employee and manager are acting in good faith, I will then tell the manager about the conversation so he can personally reassure the employee that he was heard. I will only act on the employee's recommendation when I believe that the manager in charge has failed; otherwise, we can take some intermediate actions to improve communication or reduce anxiety. Unless the manager has some private agenda or the employee is not a team player, I have found this sequence of interactions leads to better communication and trust between the two individuals. The employee rarely breaks ranks again.

In short, to be successful in breaking ranks:

- Your course of action must be undeniably in the company's best interest.

- You have to make a serious attempt to get the matter resolved with your own manager and believe that your manager's behavior is not in the company's best interest. Note that his behavior may not be intentional, as he may not have the skills, or the nerve, required to address the issue.

- The manager you seek out must recognize your skill and commitment to the company.

- You have to be willing to accept that you might not win or that the manager to whom you go might be unwilling or unable to take action. In this case, you have three choices: accept the manager's explanation and do your best to meet the company's goals within the current situation, break ranks and go even higher, or pack your tent and move on. (See below.)

## Executing a Coup d'état

The term *coup d'état* is typically applied to a military takeover that removes the people currently in power. For the purposes of this discussion, we include an attempt by one or more people to undermine your value or position in the company. We all know people who don't like us, just as we don't like certain people ourselves. The question becomes how much energy someone puts in discrediting or defeating those they don't like. Most of the time people are content to merely gossip about the person in question since talk requires the least effort and entails the least risk.

A coup d'état is usually undertaken only when the leader firmly believes that the individual(s) attacked are dangerous to their own goals or desires. Note that the leader's goals may or may not actually be in the company's best interest, but when they are not, there is a good chance the leader believes that they are. (How many people look at themselves in the bathroom mirror and think, "Gosh, I'm a great self-serving bastard."?) As a result, even if they are wrong, the leaders of an insurrection will have convinced themselves that they are operating, if not for the general good, at least for the good of some important faction.

The issue then is to discover how the leaders of a coup gain momentum and support. Just as there is an infinite variety of types of communication, there are numerous ways that people build toward a coup d'état. Your challenge is to uncover their game plan well before they strike. This area is where most of us fail because at the heart of every coup d'état is someone working from inside the existing power structure whom, chances are, you trust (at some level at least). Frequently, it is someone who hoped that you would anoint her as your successor. When that person senses that she is being passed over, she nurses the slight by magnifying your every shortcoming until she convinces herself and then many of her coworkers that you are unworthy. To build toward a coup she can use several techniques, one of which is to stage events where you exhibit the very behavior that she characterizes as dangerous. In Shakespeare's *Othello,* for example, Iago stages several scenes where Desdemona appears to be romantically involved with another man in order to provoke Othello's jealous behavior that leads to her death.

In my own case, the employee who led the palace revolt, S, used my own anger against me. In her role as manager, S would complain to me about employee X or employee Y. Trusting her, I would voice my frustration, which S would then recount to the employee while reassuring him that she had stood up for him. As a result, over time a number of people had begun to see me as a harridan (or even the pawn of my co-founder Robin) and S as the only one who cared about them. Preoccupied by raising money and worrying about revenue, I had not been spending the one-on-one time with the employees in S's department, and I did not suspect her because she had previously shown such commitment to the company and affection for me. As a result, by the time I realized what was going on, it was too late to block her behind the scenes. She had too much momentum, and I had too little credibility within her faction.

For a coup to work, the intended target of the coup must trust the leader; otherwise, it is difficult for the leader to get sufficient information to orchestrate the interactions required to gain the troops' backing. While occasionally a sociopath may be the leader of a coup, it is far more likely that the leader once looked up to the manager in question and is leading the attack for one of two reasons—either because she believes that her loyalty or performance has not been sufficiently recognized and rewarded or because she is convinced that the manager is not operating in the company's best interest.

If you are going to lead a coup d'état, you need an accurate assessment of what targets must be taken to win, you must prepare as stealthily as possible, and you have to execute your plan quickly and cleanly. S's goal—to prove my unfairness and her worth—was more emotional. Her strategy was to position herself as the developers' protector against my lack of concern and appreciation and to make me feel that she would hold me hostage if I did not give her the position she wanted. I recognized, on the one hand, that many of the people she had recruited were weak and not performing particularly well anyway (although one of the best programmers became her fiercest supporter). On the other hand, some of the team's best individuals were the types of people who were uncomfortable with infighting and conflict; they just wanted it to go away.

Finally, convinced that S's behavior was putting the company at risk, I fired her. She marshaled her resources to attack on two fronts: S had one of the company's most talented, but gullible, employees lead a campaign to discredit me with the Board and to convince as many developers to quit as possible. The five to six months it took for the company to recover from these events was excruciating. I felt violated and hurt that someone for whom I had had such affection and trust could so dislike me, guilty and worried that I had somehow misled her in what I thought of her skills, and ashamed that I was thought of as an unfair and cruel person. However, in spite of being awash in these negative feelings, I knew that S's efforts at creating a lack of trust between the development team and upper management were inherently bad for the company.

While S failed in her coup, I have seen CEOs and presidents, as well as managers and other employees, toppled in business when some trusted member of upper management has managed to discredit the targeted leader with the Board or investors. When the coup's executive has gained a commitment from the parties in power prior to any action, its execution can be clean and quick. With sufficient power behind the coup's leader, a broad base of people can be aware of what's happening with little chance of alerting the intended target. For example, when ETI was in the Austin Technology Incubator, I learned three weeks in advance from one of the managers there that the CEO of another incubator company was going to be replaced by his Board. On one level, I thought it was shameful that this information had leaked this way (and I was glad that they weren't my investors); on the other hand, there was nothing I could have done to make a difference.

A coup d'état is very difficult to pull off unless an entire organization, such as a government, is in distress or the visibility and sphere of influence of the deposed manager are already in jeopardy. If you are to lead a successful coup, you must feel secure about the following:

■ Your motivation is not based on some personal dissatisfaction but on a firm belief that the current administration is not operating in the company's best interest.

■ You must understand and have the loyalty of all key groups or, at a minimum, the group with the power required to execute the coup. While this group is usually some military or police organization in the case of a political coup, it is the Board or upper management (or a significant faction thereof) in the workplace.

■ You can move to effect the change on all fronts in as short a time period as possible.

## Mounting a Revolution

A successful coup d'état depends on the target's trust or lack of suspicion and on the perpetrator's stealth. A revolution, however, takes place over a significantly longer period of time and to be successful frequently requires support from groups not directly affected by the power structure. As a result, even if at one point the revolution's leader was initially part of the targeted management group, he must eventually detach himself from the power structure in order to publicly build support from as many people as possible.

The American Revolution or the campaign to end apartheid in South Africa are two examples of successful geopolitical revolutions. The movie *Norma Rae* told the story of how a typical revolution in business might evolve. In this particular case, fabric mills were unfairly exploiting the rural population in the South. Union organizers from outside began to distribute leaflets to inform the workers of their rights. Management became even more oppressive, threatening any workers who spoke to the union representatives. Finally one woman, Norma Rae, became irritated enough to stand up and speak out. The rest of the movie dwells on the long set of confrontations that finally led to the workers voting to establish a union.

A revolution has many stages. To be successful, you must prepare for the following:

***Creating an Initial Awareness of the Problem.*** Usually the wrong being righted by a revolution is so long-standing that the people in power ignore the oppressed's initial attempts to voice objections to the problem. ("Oh, they are demonstrating for higher wages again.") It's hard to say what finally makes the message spark in people's minds. Sometimes it might be an awareness of a similar condition being solved in another part of the world. For example, people had been writing and speaking about the injustice of South Africa's apartheid policies for decades, but it was only in 1985 that the protests received sufficient notice, in the wake of the Soweto riots, to goad the United Nations to impose an arms embargo. Subsequent economic sanctions finally created enough internal pressure within the country to cause the government to abolish the practice.

***Guerrilla Attacks on the Establishment's Representatives.*** Since the individuals in power usually ignore early protests, the instigators of a revolution must increase their visibility. Whether it's terrorist attacks or repeated and increasingly hostile coverage in the press, the assaults must escalate until the party in power feels sufficiently irritated to react. For greater impact, the assaults should enrage its victims or contain some element of surprise to make the establishment overreact when it doubts its ability to protect itself.

***Identification of the Leader(s).*** As anyone who has ever tried to conduct a meeting with more than fifteen people knows, it takes one or more strong emotional leaders to galvanize large numbers of people and move them to action. Consequently, a

**123**

key to success in a revolution is the relatively early emergence of one or more individuals who help crystallize the message and have the charisma and strong presence to give the followers hope that the revolution can succeed. In Cuba it was Ernesto "Che" Guevara and Fidel Castro, in South Africa it was Nelson Mandela, in Chiapas it is Subcomandante Marcos, and in the fabric mills of the South it was Norma Rae. The leader of a revolution helps the beneficiaries of the revolution recognize that their plight is unjust and intolerable. He inspires the revolutionaries, serving as their spokesperson to the outside community. As a result, the leader of a revolution must be brave, for he often experiences hardship: persecution, imprisonment, or even martyrdom.

*Retribution.* Just as someone who has been brushing a fly away in annoyance will use far more force than required when she finally has an opportunity to strike, the targets of a revolution will eventually react with such force that they both lose the sympathy of bystanders and further galvanize the revolutionaries. And just like the person reacting to the fly, the intensity of their reaction is not intentional, but emotional. As indicated above, frequently the parties in power do not recognize the onset of the revolution since the abuses being addressed by the revolution are typically long-standing and accompanied by periodic, if not regular, protests. Hence, initially those in power tend to ignore the revolutionary's efforts, much like one almost unconsciously brushes away a fly. However, as the revolutionary assaults increase, the parties in power become concerned that they are being undermined and will begin to escalate their response. In geopolitical circles, this counterattack may entail the arrest of the "usual suspects"; in business, they fire or demote one or more of the more active revolutionaries.

When the forces are in place to conduct a successful revolution, rather than discouraging the revolutionaries, these acts of retribution actually spur them on until at some point the frequency or brutality of their assaults gets some attention. And after the parties in power finally are sufficiently irritated, they act with what they hope will be enough brutality to discourage the insurgency, but they usually create one or more martyrs whom the revolutionaries can use to further incense the masses.

***Escalation of Cycle of Events toward Denouement.*** The cycle of guerrilla attacks and retribution continues until one of two things happens—the parties in power react with enough force to contain the revolution or the revolutionaries gain sufficient backing to overthrow the power structure. In the case of Norma Rae and the fabric mills, the union was established, and many of the managers in charge were removed from power.

Few people in business seek to mount a revolution for a number of reasons:

- The amount of effort, time, and people required—as well as the potential for collateral damage (for example, being fired)—entails far more work and risk than most of us are willing to undertake. Remember that most successful revolutions entail sacrificing one or two martyrs to the cause.

- Success often leads to restructuring, which has a whole new set of problems that hamper the company's ultimate success.

## Packing Your Tent

If you believe that the problems you face within your company would take a revolution to solve, you might be better off packing your tent and moving on. The alternatives are staying in an environment where you are extremely unhappy or taking on all the risks and commitment required to revolt. There are two major ways that people "pack their tent," one of which leads to more personal growth than the other. If you simply dismiss the organization as totally awful and go off to find a new job believing that no other company could be as bad, odds are that in a few years you'll be equally disappointed in your next position. Companies are like marriages, and none of them are easy. The parties involved may have widely different talents and circumstances, and this pair may have money or a great sex life while that pair may not. Whenever you have groups of people who depend on each other for their success in the world, there will be problems.

Consequently, a more productive way to pack your tent is to take the time to examine what has made you unhappy and actively seek a new position that gives you a chance to avoid those particular frustrations in the future. When Rod Canion and his fellow employees at Texas Instruments became convinced that TI was making a terrible decision by not making its first personal computer compatible with the IBM PC, they left to found Compaq Computer and went on to new battles and great victories. After seven years of programming experience at TI and MCC, where I had no say over where my efforts would be focused, I decided that I would take another systems programming job only as a last resort. It wasn't just a matter of my bad luck (so to speak) with bosses. I also hated the fact that so often the company wasn't sufficiently committed to success and dropped projects rather than push them through, wasting my efforts and those of everyone else.

What I wanted was to work on a product that would bring value—and therefore have a market—and to do whatever necessary to get that product to the marketplace. With a proposal in hand, I went to different MCC managers to procure some exploratory funding. People found it interesting and were polite, but they usually wound up suggesting that I talk to someone else. With my reputation as a firebrand, I was aware that behind their polite behavior, they were probably thinking,

"No way I'm taking on a management nightmare like you, lady." (At the time I promised myself that I would never be so angry or indiscreet in expressing my frustration and provide someone with that excuse again.) Finally, Gene Lowenthal gave us a break and the money to start the project. Each subsequent success has led to a new challenge and another battle, and the lessons learned make up this book.

In short, if done correctly, the decision to pack your tent can be one of the most invigorating decisions you can make in your professional life. For that to happen, you must honestly assess not only what you dislike about the environment you are leaving, but what you dislike about how you have behaved in that environment. Then you must concentrate on eliminating both sources of frustration in your next position. The important thing in changing your behavior is stepwise progress, however. I could no more have rooted the anger out of my personality immediately upon leaving the CAD program than I could have transformed myself into an ascetic (and that ain't ever going to happen). What I could do is understand that expressing that anger with that level of intensity in a professional environment was counterproductive and then try to avoid that behavior, particularly around potential enemies.

By the way, it has taken almost ten years, but anger is no longer one of my dominant emotions. I have learned to show it, to effect, without feeling it because it can be a useful tool. But when on rare occasions I do get really angry, it exhausts me, and I wonder how I survived so many years with that much negative emotion. Then I remember that anger is the mask of fear, and I feel sorry for that woman I used to be who was so afraid.

### Withstanding a Direct Assault

In the previous sections, we have focused on characterizing different modes of battle you can use to achieve your goal. In this section, I want to focus on what you should consider when you are the target of an attack. Often one of your biggest challenges is recognizing that you are under assault before the damage is done—before you have been politicked out of a promotion or the Board has voted to fire you. Usually detecting this situation is difficult because the assault comes from someone you either have trusted or want to trust. One of the earliest signs that you may be under attack is that you feel hurt because someone doesn't understand you or has misjudged you. The natural reaction is to try to convince that person that he or she is mistaken. If you succeed, you should have a new level of understanding with the person, and this type of incident shouldn't reoccur. If you do not succeed or you find yourself weeks later in a similar conflict, it's time to step back and consider what the other person's issues might be.

For example, when I worked for a boss named B, I often felt like he didn't like or understand me. Whenever I made a point, even if he didn't disagree, he would still diminish it, citing one or more ways about how the company worked that I simply didn't understand. While people will always tell you not to take something personally to quell your anger, my problem was that I didn't take his disparagement personally. I knew that I was a bright, if inexperienced, and committed employee. I figured he must not have understood me. Furthermore, I wanted to trust him, because he was my boss. In the case of S, the employee of whom I was enormously fond but who tried to lead a coup against me, it was even harder. I already trusted her. I wanted affection and loyalty in return.

With both my boss and S, I was regularly frustrated in my interactions with each of them. However, instead of acknowledging my discomfort, stepping back from what I wanted, and analyzing the other person dispassionately, I focused on what I had said or done to have misled them. As a result, I tortured myself about why my boss B didn't understand that I was trying to be a good employee and had the company's best interest at heart. Because I was genuinely fond of S, with her case I told myself that she had overreacted. In other words, in both cases I gave the other person the benefit of the doubt, long before I trusted my own instincts, and I suffered for a significantly longer time as a result. Ultimately, I had to go to great lengths to withstand their assaults. I finally had to "gain a commission" by going around B and had to block a coup d'état in the case of S.

The lesson to be learned here is that you deserve as much respect as anyone else. If your interactions with others make you uncomfortable, a good part of the problem likely lies with them as much as with you. So give yourself a break. Step back, look at their motivation, test your hypotheses. You may discover that they themselves are not aware of their behavior or motivation, in which case it is even more important that you accurately assess the situation and act sooner instead of later. Moreover, you must act decisively, for it is easier to discourage someone from negative behavior before it has become habitual or before they have convinced themselves that they are justified in their reactions to you. (S: "Kay gets so angry at people; it's lucky that I'm here to protect people from her.") I am reminded of what my horseback riding teacher told me about using a whip. My initial instinct was to hit the horse lightly, as a warning. My instructor immediately corrected me, telling me that a horse was tough and that I had to make the whip hurt when I first used it, or it would have no effect as a threat. In other words, to discourage misbehaving, there must be no doubt in the horse's mind that you mean business.

It is also important not to underestimate the damage that a single individual's ill will can cause. More than twenty years ago, when he was seventeen, my good friend R had immigrated to the United States from a developing country to go to college. Since that time he has remained active in his ethnic community and is the kind of person who might be interrupted at dinner by an elderly friend who doesn't speak English to call and describe the chest pains she was having to her doctor. Because he was so well respected in his community, when he started a high-tech company in 1989, many members of the community sought to invest. He wound up raising approximately $900,000 from almost forty investors, not realizing that this ownership structure would discourage venture capital investment. As a result, he never had the capital that would allow him to perform his research and development (R&D) activity at the desired rate, even after having raised another $600,000 from a group of wealthy investors, also from his culture. However, he persevered, even though it meant funding the company for seven months with his credit cards and running up a $50,000 debt. He was able to survive only because he was single and had previously purchased several pieces of real estate, the rental income from which covered part of his living expenses.

Finally, he was close enough to a product to be able to borrow $200,000 from a business angel. With that money, he completed a prototype of the product, which allowed him to raise a little more than $300,000 from another group in exchange for an exclusive right to sell and distribute the product for a fixed period. As the first products began to ship and revenues came in the door, R began to draw his salary and relax, believing that he finally had a chance to return value to the people who had trusted in him. Tired of living in the windowless condo he had bought while he was student, R listed his property, reclaimed some of the back salary owed him, and bought a 2,700-square-foot house.

Unfortunately, one of his Board members was a "friend" named F whose own business was not doing well. It irked F that R was buying a new house while F still had money tied up in the company and had no date at which he could be assured he would get his money back. Despite the fact that one of a Board member's primary obligations is to prevent shareholder unrest (while ensuring that the company is being run ethically), F began to lobby other shareholders who were his friends that they should get some kind of personal guarantee from R that they would get their money back if the company failed. In the meantime, he also began to call R on an almost daily basis to tell him some of the older shareholders were really suffering and needed their money. F even told him that some shareholders thought R had bought the new house then because he knew the company was going to fold and in the event he had to declare bankruptcy, his interest in the house would be protected. This argument showed how little F understood about R's liability. As a founder, president, and major stockholder in the company, R was not liable for the company's debts, and he had only obtained from the company the salary owed him so he had no debt to the company.

However, rather than proactively addressing these concerns with the shareholders, R focused on how bad he felt that he couldn't predict when (or even if) his investors could cash out and that they would think that he wasn't always putting their interests first. He even talked to an investment banker to see if he could raise money to buy out the initial investors. The banker had indicated it might be possible with six months of strong revenue growth and as long as the initial investors were willing to settle for a moderate time-based return on their money or to place their shares in a voting trust. However, at no time during this period did R seek to halt F's behavior to address F's concerns with the shareholders.

With each week, F became bolder, finally hiring a lawyer and accusing R in a letter to the shareholders of misappropriating company funds. He even convinced the other Board members to cut R's pay in half, thereby violating the terms and conditions of an employment contract the last round of investors had insisted R sign. After $10,000 in legal fees, R was able to clear his name, but in the meantime he had lost four months in precious R&D time working on specific product adaptations requested by several manufacturers who wanted to serve as OEMs for his product. (OEMs are original equipment manufacturers, companies that buy your components to embed or incorporate them into their products.) Cash was again becoming tight, and with the company's troubled history, R's chances for engaging the banker to raise additional funds had been significantly reduced. At this time, it is unclear whether the company can recover. The irony, of course, is that the investors had already come so close to losing their investment and then they allowed F to attack when it appeared that the company had a chance to succeed. And it all stemmed from jealousy about R's buying a house. (It seems that F's wife had been wanting a new house, but he had not been in a position to buy one.)

In short, you should neither underestimate the damage that a single individual can cause nor assume that people will not act against their own self-interest if their emotions are clouding their judgment. When you are troubled by the actions or reactions of another person whom you trust or want to trust, you must remove yourself from your own emotional reaction, assess whether that individual's actions are in the best interest of the company, and if not, act early and decisively. The longer you wait the more costly it becomes to remedy the situation—if indeed, it is even still possible.

## Readiness for Battle

The goal of this chapter has been to help outline when and how you can go to battle as well as to discuss the factors you should assess in determining if the battle is justified. Key to making the right decision is being able to recognize what you are afraid of because fear is usually at the root of any intense reaction to a situation. Once you are convinced that a situation merits engaging in conflict, review the above descriptions of different modes of battle to determine the factors that characterize your own situation in terms of the risk and the enemies you face. This exercise should help you decide which mode of battle is appropriate to use. The following chapters will help you develop tactics to implement your strategy.

## Notes

1. Frank Herbert, *Dune* (New York: Ace Books, 1965).

2. H. A. Guerber, *Myths of the Norsemen: From the Eddas and Sagas* (New York: Dover, 1992).

3. J. A. Fodor, T. G. Bever, and M. F. Garrett, *The Psychology of Language* (New York: McGraw-Hill, 1974).

4. Serge King, *Mastering Your Hidden Self—A Guide to the Huna Way* (Wheaton, Ill.: Quest, 1985).

5. Ibid., p. 35.

6. Loki was one of the principal Norse gods who was often the cause of dissension among the other gods. He is characterized as a contriver of discord and mischief.

# Acquiring Allies
## How to Gain Support

The human is a creature of paradox. No sooner does a man embrace a woman or a position than some nagging fear makes him worry this best thing could be bested by another. As a result, we spend an enormous amount of our interactions with others seeking validation of our perceptions. We ask, Can you believe that she had the nerve to ask him if he was cheating on his wife? Isn't it outrageous how he yells at his subordinates? Did you see the look on her face when she realized that somebody else got the promotion?

Any conflict involves risk, and with risk comes fear. Humans have always banded together to reduce risk, whether in battling the elements or each other. As a result, it is understandable that soliciting allies or seeking support is a common tactic for those about to do battle. However, too often the would-be warrior assumes that verbal support means support in battle, when, in fact, too much focus on obtaining verbal support can actually slow the speed at which people join his cause and help. This chapter explores techniques for recognizing when you are trying to acquire allies for the wrong purpose, what you reasonably can expect from allies in the workplace, and how you can go about getting the help you need.

## Whose Battle Is It Anyway?

Because seeking verbal support is such a common way of helping ourselves feel comfortable with uncertainty, it is not surprising that we also consider it a good means to acquire allies. If
someone agrees with us, we assume that they will back us in
battle. In fact, because we have this mistaken assumption, we
tend to become even more outspoken and heated when talking about the injustice or bad judgment we oppose, as if our
intensity will trigger the same passion in others. While we hope
our listeners will join us in arms, thereby increasing the chance
for success, the reality is that often the more heated you
become the less supportive your audience becomes. This
pulling back happens for a number of reasons:

- They do not feel the same level of commitment to the
  cause.

- They think you are overreacting.

- They believe that you may cause them damage in
  others' eyes.

### Commitment to the Cause

Remember, frequently the reason for going to battle is as personal as it is public. For example, you may have worked on
enough badly managed projects in your company that you
would rather quit than see another project fail, and because
your feelings are intense, you are willing to risk enemies, or
even being fired, to see if you can cause a change in the management structure. However, just because you might be willing
to face calling a headhunter or combing the want ads, that
doesn't mean that your buddy, Bill, feels the same way. His
wife might be ill, or he might be in debt, or he might just not
care as much as you do. So while your friends at work enjoy

"dissin'" the boss from time to time, they might be less than enthused when you describe what you intend to do and even colder and more noncommittal if you want to include them in your plans.

## Impression of Overreacting

Because we rarely undertake a battle unless we believe the cost of not acting is severe, the would-be warrior is usually emotional and intense when discussing the injustices she wishes to right. In fact, the more symbolic the battle is on a personal level the more emotion and intensity the warrior will convey. And the potential ally will reach the correct conclusion—that the warrior is taking the situation personally, and as such, her perceptions are suspect. This description was certainly true of me when I worked in the computer-aided design program at MCC. Previously at Texas Instruments, where my sharp tongue and intensity earned me a fairly bad reputation, I didn't get personal when I complained, but instead remained focused on what the company needed to do to be successful. Although I didn't attract many allies, I was effective.

At MCC, I was different. Part of what provoked my indiscreet behavior was the general working climate. MCC was both the worst and the best environment I have ever worked in. It was the best because of its lofty goals and upper management's commitment to providing its researchers with the best possible working environment. No expense was spared. We had superior hardware, an information center with runners who would seek out the books and articles you needed, a cafeteria with linens and flowers on the table and excellent food at minimum cost, and great health and retirement benefits.

One would think that such an environment would have bred loyalty and excellence, but it didn't. Instead, it engendered a culture of self-importance and contempt. Too often the researchers who already had strong international reputations took the stance that they were finally getting the treatment their work deserved and demanded more and not less, regardless of the cost. One might need a condo and car in San Jose since it was simply not possible to attract enough technical talent to Austin to perform the necessary work. Another insisted that an entire team of seven researchers had to go to a conference in France rather than just one or two. These demands were exacerbated by the fact that MCC had a sizable annual bonus pool that management awarded to programs and groups within each program based on the previous year's perceived success. While this incentive program might have done wonders in a company where employees' loyalty and focus were on furthering the company's business, it lead to backbiting and vilification in MCC's culture of self-promotion.

Because everyone was acting out, I began to focus on my enemies' personal weaknesses as much as on what I believed they were doing wrong. And it was easy to do. One of my bosses publicly emphasized his role in the community: as a deacon in his church, as active in the schools, as a pillar of society. Yet from my point of view he was extremely mean-spirited and had a terrible attitude toward women. (In fact, MCC was hard on female researchers. During my years there our ranks grew to eighty, only to dwindle to a dozen or so by the time I left.) And as I mentioned earlier, this boss also made it clear that hiring me wasn't his idea in my initial interview.

His behavior was offensive to many people, but unlike other people, who may have just made jokes at his expense, I felt offended by his very existence. Why did I have such a strong reaction? Perhaps it was because once again—after my father and then my husband—I was at the mercy of someone I perceived to be an irrational and dishonest man. So when I sought to attract allies, rather than concentrating on the technical and tactical issues that would have united us, I focused on the man. As a result, my audience discredited most of what I said because they quite rightly thought that I was overreacting.

## Fear of Personal Damage

Colleagues frequently become uncomfortable when you push them for a commitment or appear to be launching a vendetta, but they can treat you like a leper if you have publicly gone to war and are at risk politically. In this case, they are afraid that any association they have with you may put them at risk as well. I encountered this situation when I did battle at Texas Instruments. As discussed earlier, close to the beginning of my second year, I was assigned as technical lead and later the manager of the hand-off of a natural language prototype from the research lab in Dallas. It was an excellent piece of work, but because it had been developed as a prototype no one had given any thought to the development environment needed to support the technology as a product. However, senior management at TI was so impressed that they simply had to demonstrate its capability at the launch of the TI PC at a tradeshow in December.

As a result, that August I was given a team of six programmers, three IBM PCs (since the TI PCs were still at the engineering model stage), and a deadline. The original prototype was written in the Lisp programming language but the new application was to be delivered in C, two languages that none of us knew. To help us understand the algorithm behind the prototype, one of the Dallas researchers—who knew Lisp but not C—wrote a version of the prototype in Pascal, a language with which many of us had experience. This project was highly visible and almost impossible given the time line and our lack of equipment. To make it worse, we had a terrible relationship with the researchers from the lab. They thought that mere programmers from Austin couldn't possibly contribute to the design, so whenever we brought up a design question, they would tell us to "go do our coding" and they would get back to us when they had an answer. This attitude was insulting, especially considering that a number of people on our team had had design responsibility on commercial products. Moreover, the guys at the lab were extremely concerned that we wouldn't make the deadline to showcase their work.

In some respects, the "we/they" attitudes—"We'll show them" and all that—may have served to bind my team emotionally. It also resulted in a lot of friction and—you guessed it—I was at the center of most of it. I battled with the lab to get the dialogue we needed to understand what we were trying to build, and I battled with my boss to get *him* to do battle for additional hardware so we didn't have to work in shifts. During this period, I was at my most strident. I called them like I saw them, but I became increasingly isolated. As I offended more and more people in relatively high positions, some of my more ambitious colleagues began to avoid me for fear that some of management's hostility for me might be transferred to them. At the time I judged my coworkers harshly. (Why should they be different from anyone else?) Now I understand. It was my battle. I had chosen to fight it; they hadn't. It wasn't reasonable to expect others to risk injury when it wasn't their fight. As it turned out, we made the deadline, received great recognition, and evolved into a twelve-person team with great esprit de corps.

## Recognize That It Is Your Battle

There are two rewards for successfully taking on risk—making something outside yourself better and improving yourself. Prolonged public testimony and outcry are only suitable when you are trying to mount a revolution. Consequently, if you find yourself communicating this way to acquire allies, stop and ask yourself if revolution is your goal or if you are seeking to reduce your fear. If it is the latter, find another way to do it. I personally have found a combination of therapy and friends to have been enormously helpful over the years—therapists because of their distance and perspective and friends because of their affection and common history, which helps them evaluate your insights. But in the end your ultimate ally is that person looking back at you from the bathroom mirror.

## So How Do You Acquire Allies?

Just because it is unrealistic to think that you can gain a commitment from allies before the war has begun, don't underestimate their importance to your success. At the outset, it is probably better to think of colleagues as pawns rather than soldiers committed to fighting on your behalf. If they see you are actually fighting for a good cause and if you make the right moves, they are likely to turn into soldiers.

There are actually four steps to acquiring effective allies:

- identify potential allies,

- set the stage and gather intelligence,

- plant a filter, and

- ask for action.

However, before proceeding it is important to point out that at one level the following sections may seem to advise you to be manipulative, almost Machiavellian, in the way you interact with colleagues. At some level, they do. There is no point in going to war if you don't intend to win; otherwise, you risk your own well-being and that of those you care about by almost assuredly failing. Therefore, if you choose to fight, you owe it to yourself and to those who depend on you to proceed in a way that maximizes your chance of success. Remember also, though, that your opportunities to prevail will be enhanced only if your goal is worthy, because "might makes right" has less impact in workplace warfare than on the physical battleground. With this idea in mind, consider how to achieve the following goals on your own particular battleground.

## Identify Potential Allies

To be successful in war you must assess where your enemy can cause you damage and choose allies from the right mix of people who can help you in these arenas. If you are afraid that your supervisor has it in for you, it might be emotionally gratifying to enlist the emotional support of your neighbor or your friend who works in another department, but it's not likely that they will be of much use to you. Ideally, you should identify four to eight people who have contact with your enemy on a variety of levels: for example, one or more of his peers, someone above him in the organization, one or two colleagues at your level, and perhaps one or two people from other organizations within the company. Note that it is important that you choose people who are well respected, or the impact of their help will be diminished. If you don't already have relationships with these people, you must build them.

In some cases you may want the relationship to have a social element, such as lunch or coffee, but usually not outside of office hours with families or it will be hard for you to have serious and candid conversations. (Of course, having a family-oriented gathering is fine, as long as you have enough one-on-one time to have candid, private conversations.) When the person holds a higher position in the firm, you may find it hard to develop the relationship, as she may not have the time or believe it appropriate to spend significant one-on-one time with you. However, upper management will likely be involved because you must let someone at that level know about what you are trying to achieve and why you believe it is important. That is enough at the early stages.

In my own case, when my research project in the CAD program was canceled and I realized how few allies I had in what was essentially an unfair battle (one of the instigators told me, years later, how bad he had felt about his behavior), it became clear that my behavior—not my cause—had alienated people. I vowed never to make the same mistake again, and although I may have in some form, it has not been with the intensity of the past. (I relapse, sort of like an ex-smoker who breaks down time and again.) I decided to present only a measured and rational face to others and to keep my judgments about others to myself.

After the CAD project, T and I were assigned to what we believed was a doomed effort to build an object-oriented database management system. We both justifiably believed that our reassignment would make it easy to put us in the first wave of layoffs after it failed and the program finally had to be cut back. Once we had hatched the idea for ETI's flagship product and determined that neither of us had the resources to develop a company outside of the normal workday, I could not bear the thought of another systems programmer's job and devised a plan to get an independent research project funded to pursue the work. Our odds of succeeding were not good. For one, I did not have the stature of most of the lead researchers at MCC. In fact, many of them sneered that the EXTRACT project, as it was called at MCC, was not *real* research. Also, I was considered a loose cannon with a hot temper and a big mouth.

However, I figured that the worst I could do was fail, so I wrote a proposal, asked various researchers and program heads to review it, and incorporated their comments. Then I began to ask people to fund it. Some of these people I had consulted during the proposal writing—people like Lyle Welty, who had run the parallel processing program for a period and was beginning to head up a group responsible for obtaining government funding. Others were new, such as John Pinkston, the chief scientist who had his own fund for exploratory research, or Gene Lowenthal, who once had his own database company but at that time was the vice president for the Advanced Computing Technology Program. In all cases, however, I never brought up my previous problems in the CAD program or mentioned the enemies whom I had allowed to provoke me into such previously foolhardy behavior. Occasionally, as some of us became friendly, they would bring up what they had heard, and I would indirectly acknowledge that I believed the CAD program was in trouble and that I had perhaps behaved inadvisably. I never dwelled on the topic or told old war stories to avoid resurrecting fears about my being too emotional.

In monitoring my behavior, I learned three valuable lessons. First, anger is probably one of our most permanent—and valuable—enemies, and containing it is critical prior to going to war. The second is that we all have the opportunity for redefining how we interact with the world and a chance for redemption. I have made the following point about anger before and cannot overemphasize how important it is: When you feel anger, there are always two enemies—one is the person or group you are mad at; the other is spawned by fear. Until you understand that fear, you will be less effective in dealing with your enemy. Moreover, you never fully vanquish this internal enemy, but you may learn to contain it in one form. For example, I rarely display, or even feel, my anger in the way I once did. I have learned to bank it, like a fire. But I occasionally have to stop myself and reexamine, particularly if I have felt some rage for a period of time, what I am afraid of and whether I am correctly assessing my objective in some battle. The final lesson is that people feel their anger differently. In my case, I feel a rush of adrenaline, and my heartbeat increases. Other people shut down and become depressed. You must learn to detect the signs that tell you that some battle must be fought, if only with your internal demons. This recognition, in turn, will make you more effective when identifying your allies.

### Set the Stage and Gather Intelligence

In chapter 3 we discussed how observing people's communication styles can give you an insight as to whether they would be trustworthy allies. Once you have identified the individuals you think you could trust as potential allies, then you should spend your initial time with them gathering information. Rather than holding forth about what you believe is wrong and what should be done to fix it, ask them questions and volunteer information only to support some point they make or to suggest something they might want to think about. For example, rather than saying, "If they put Dr. R in charge of the program, it'll be like working in a concentration camp" (which leaves no doubt about where you stand), it would be better to ask, "Do you think that they are going to put Dr. R in charge of the program? I've heard that he can be difficult."

The merit to this approach is twofold. First, it allows you to find out (some of) what this person knows and believes. (Not everyone is totally forthcoming.) Next, it registers your concern and allows you to articulate some of what you know without making it clear how emotionally invested you are. If the individual expresses some sympathy or concern regarding your feelings on the topic, they will likely become an additional pair of eyes and ears working on your behalf. The next time you have lunch or coffee and the topic comes up—frequently your potential ally will actually broach the topic—he will likely tell you what he has observed or heard. In short, this stage is devoted to understanding and preparing the person to be your ally.

Only after I had established trust and friendship with the allies I had cultivated to support my efforts at getting funding for the EXTRACT project did I begin to share my fears about having to go to war. As is the case in most sales cycles, many potential investors were interested, but it was hard to get anyone to sign a check. When evaluating the initial proposal, most individuals suggested other people whom I should seek out in part as a way of encouraging me to ask for money elsewhere, no doubt. One of these individuals, a Dr. F, was a world-renowned researcher whose own work had potential synergy with the proposed research. He was quite supportive of the value of the research but consistently said he had no money. In many ways,

Dr. F and I were alike. He also had a reputation for being difficult to deal with and was feuding with his boss. As a result, many of my closer allies would also caution me when they advised me to talk to him; the closest even mentioned that we appeared to have the same temperament. As it turned out, the vice president who eventually gave us our initial funds, with the understanding that we would seek additional funding from the context of Dr. F's lab, warned me that he was not sure that Dr. F and I would get along. So I was repeating a previous negative pattern and going to work for someone with whom I would likely go to war.

This time it was different, however; I didn't care about Dr. F's character. My goals were to secure funding for the project and to make it successful. Moreover, for the first year or so, Dr. F and I had an excellent relationship, treating each other with respect. With his support, we obtained three corporate sponsors within the first six months, each committing to funding $150,000 a year for 1989 and 1990. It was only after the EXTRACT project began to receive more visibility in its own right that problems began to arise. Dr. F did not see anything particularly revolutionary in what we were doing. Other researchers had already created one such system but without an extensible architecture. (On the other hand, if it had been obvious to everyone how to build such a system, we wouldn't have pursued it.) Dr. F thought, however, that he could use the results of our project in his next major work, a concept not in keeping with my vision of founding a company to take the research to the marketplace. I realized within approximately a year that at some point Dr. F and I would have to go to war, but unlike in the past, I wanted to avoid a confrontation until I had no other choice. As a result, we coexisted comfortably until I began to deal with one of his avowed enemies, a director of marketing named N.

Like many talented scientists, Dr. F had little respect for sales and marketing, which in many ways led to the failure of a company he started after leaving MCC. Moreover, the individual in question was flamboyant and irreverent, or antithetical in style to Dr. F. As it turned out, however, N and his people were very interested in working with the EXTRACT team, in part because our work addressed a large problem that cost the research sponsors millions of dollars a year. As a result, given the comparatively low cost of participation in the research project (that was a strategy as well, as I was not a renowned researcher), it was relatively easy to spark interest in our project even as the MCC shareholders were facing difficult financial times. But Dr. F was not pleased. First of all, he had publicly gone to war with N, and here was one of his lieutenants consorting with the enemy. Second, as the visibility of the EXTRACT project increased, Dr. F began to think that I might be less than willing to fold the results of our work into his next project. This discomfort caused him to draw the line. He called me into his office, told me to focus on my research and not waste my time with N. He declared he would interact with N for all the projects in his lab. There it was. If I didn't interact with N, then I had little chance of obtaining the additional funding or visibility I needed to form a start-up. If I did work with N, I would be disobeying a direct order from a supervisor who brooked no insubordination. Clearly I was going to have to go to war, so I took the offensive and planted a filter.

## Plant a Filter

Physical combat is often more straightforward than battle in the workplace. In the workplace, many of the most lethal assaults are launched when you are not present, so you must plant your defenses before they occur. I call this "planting a filter." Earlier in this chapter, we focused on how important it is when acquiring allies that you appear to be somewhat dispassionate and objective while getting them to articulate their concerns about the situation so you can volunteer your opinions in support of theirs. If you have conducted this dialogue effectively before you go to war and if what you are trying to achieve is just or in the common good, it is relatively easy to build strong defenses by alerting your allies that trouble may be coming.

Once again, the key is to minimize any expression of anger while you tell your ally that you fear the enemy may try to attack. You will need to lend credibility to this claim by describing a conversation or argument you had or a series of actions you have observed. Moreover, you should never refer to your opponent as an enemy or even an opponent, because when the enemy attacks, you want your ally to see for himself that the enemy's behavior is unjust and dishonest. This approach plants a filter in your ally's mind so that he carefully considers anything your enemy says to him about you or your situation. In short, he will question every opinion your enemy tries to impress on him and, in so doing, come to feel protective of you.

Note that this affinity does not mean that your ally will actually directly confront the enemy or openly declare his loyalty to you. Remember, you have already recognized that other people probably will not want to assume the same level of risk that you will, so the best you can probably hope for when engaging the enemy is that your ally will be noncommittal or refuse to act. However, you can expect that your ally will discuss the dynamics of your conflict with others and as several of these incidents become known (your enemy will likely attack you on several fronts), your allies will become even more committed to support you. Further, if your enemy is stupid enough to lie, and that lie comes to light in your allies' discussions, your allies will probably act on your behalf.

I first consciously planted a filter in my situation with Dr. F. Because my goal was to spin out a company if our research project was sufficiently successful at MCC, it was important to attract a sufficient number of research sponsors and to have the EXTRACT project be regarded as successful. As a result, I felt it was critical that I cooperate with N, the head of marketing. I also suspected that Dr. F wanted to keep my visibility relatively low so he would be free to use our research results if he wanted. Given Dr. F's personality, I knew that arguing with him would be futile; we were clearly going to wind up going to war. So I planted a filter with his boss, Dr. K, the vice president who had given us our exploratory funding and with whom Dr. F was already engaged in a feud. (Dr. F once confessed to me in an expansive moment that he planned to wait until Dr. K had sufficiently discredited himself and then Dr. F was sure to be offered his position.)

In a short appointment with Dr. K, I let him know that the honeymoon between Dr. F and me was over. (Dr. K had half-jokingly commented to me several times that he couldn't believe how well Dr. F and I had been getting on.) I then described the conversation we had had about N and stated that my plan was not to openly confront Dr. F. Instead I would explain to N in marketing that Dr. F had told me not to deal with him—clearly not in MCC's best interest—and to ask N to call me if he needed anything rather than come directly to my office. In this way, I could provide marketing with what they needed without arguing with Dr. F about the matter. Dr. K offered to let the project, now funded, report directly to him, but I said that for the time being I did not see the need to make the problem worse.

While you should plant a filter with the individuals who are the most likely audience for the enemy's assault, you should also inform all of your allies about each turn of events, because you need the support of popular opinion. It is important here to be subtle. In the case of your featured players, or those who are likely to be consulted directly by the enemy, you should plant the filter as quickly as possible and set up a meeting for the sole purpose of alerting them to the changing situation. In the case of your chorus, or the allies whose general support you want but who are less likely to be confronted directly by the enemy, you are better off subtly working the information into your regular conversations. You can say, "Did I tell you the latest?"

My plan for how to proceed with Dr. F went smoothly until he saw a presentation in which it was clear that N and I had been talking. Dr. F was furious and threatened to throw my project out of his lab. I didn't react directly, but I did make another appointment with Dr. K to say that perhaps it was time that the project reported directly to him. As it happened, Dr. F left for an extended business trip, and by the time he had returned, our offices were moved and Dr. K informed him of the reporting change. Dr. F was stunned, reportedly saying that it was like getting a divorce after the first fight, but he clearly wasn't going to let me get away with disobeying him. He made an appointment with the then-current CEO of MCC and told him that he must cancel the EXTRACT project because it had a fatal flaw. The CEO contacted Dr. K to ask what should be done. Dr. K, having known about the conflict between Dr. F and myself for some months and having supported my moving the project, told the CEO that Dr. F's complaints were sour grapes, and that if there actually were a fatal flaw, Dr. F should simply document it.

Obviously, several things helped me here, including Dr. F's general temperament and his previous hard feelings with Dr. K. However, I have successfully used this technique of planting a filter on other occasions, as with the senior manager I had hired at ETI who tried to undermine me with the Board. In that case, I had not actually anticipated the assault, but the technique worked anyway. Because I did not attack him but stated my fears as concerns, my ally on the Board was alerted to the potential problem and brought it up as a casual point of discussion with the other Board members as opposed to a problem they needed to address. As a result, in both cases, my refusal to attack put the enemies' behavior under a spotlight. Any claim they made was considered to be potentially hostile or destructive, and any dishonesty was recognized prior to any open conflict between the enemy and me. As a result, my allies were moved to act on my behalf.

## Ask for Action

At all times you should acknowledge that the battle is your battle and that you would not presume to ask someone else to fight it for you. Accordingly, you should ask for action from allies only after the enemy has revealed himself and even then ask for as little help as possible. For example, rather than requesting that someone go to the president and speak on your behalf, you should ask if the ally in question would mind serving as a reference should the president want to discuss the issue. If you have cultivated the right mix of allies and allowed them to observe enough of your enemies' behavior over a sufficient period, then you should have adequate resources to parcel out small, specific favors to help you along. In this way, your ally is grateful to act on your behalf, because the action itself is small and involves minimal risk or effort and yet he can feel good that he is supporting you in your battle.

In summary, winning a war in the workplace almost always requires a strong set of allies, but to be successful in acquiring allies you must remember that they are neither comrades in arms nor are they to serve as your emotional support except in the most circumspect ways. If you must express your anger, do it away from the workplace or in the company of personal friends. Take care to minimize the number of friends you use as allies for two reasons. First, to use them effectively you will have to be selective about what you show them, thereby eliminating them as a source of emotional support, and second, if they are good friends, they are probably more vividly aware of your weaknesses and faults than other colleagues and this knowledge could mitigate their perception of the enemy. Finally, the ultimate value of allies is that they can help bear witness to your trustworthiness and sense of honor, thereby decreasing the ability of others to attack you.

Many of the above techniques will work for some time even if you are dishonest and self-serving. Ultimately you will get what you deserve, so you should regularly examine your heart and your motives to see if you deserve your own respect, much less the respect and support of others.

## What Are Comrades?

Allies support your cause but do not depend on your success. With comrades, your fates are tied, and you are mutually dependent on the other's success. Just as in the case of allies, some comrades are more skilled and trustworthy than others. In the closest case, a comrade is a partner or someone with whom you trust any information. Friendships forged in the workplace can be among your most satisfying relationships. Your mutual dependence on each other breeds respect and trust, your mutual successes joy and exhilaration, and your defeats sympathy and understanding. Sometimes a partner even becomes a good personal friend, although there, as in every relationship, boundaries are important. In fact, failing to define boundaries usually leads to conflicts between comrades and sometimes to the destruction of the relationship itself.

## When a Comrade Turns against You

All relationships are temporary, whether they are professional or personal. In the best case, they last a lifetime. However, one of the hardest emotional issues you can face is when an ally becomes an enemy. Whether it's the case of a failed marriage or a failed business partnership, you not only feel loss and betrayal, but also a sense of failure. That sense of failure is usually tied to a feeling that you somehow could have stopped this dissolution if you had only recognized the signs and acted earlier. In this section, we will examine why business alliances fail, when they can be saved, or in the event that a professional divorce is required, how it can be managed.

There are three primary reasons why business alliances fail:

- You have different expectations.

- You have conflicting values.

- Your relationship is too exclusive of others.

## Different Expectations

People find it difficult to talk directly about their expectations for a variety of reasons. First, they often are afraid that people might judge them if they expect more than others think they are worth or, even worse, might be jealous if they are worthy and have a chance of reaching their goals. Thus, the individual who says, "I expect that I will be promoted to VP before the year is out" is considered either a bit odd or ill-mannered. Most of us are fairly cagey about expressing what we expect. Someone may say, "I've always dreamed about being a writer," or "What I'd give to be able to have that position for a day!" We tend to hope that people will recognize our merits and efforts, intuit what we want, and work to provide us with our just rewards.

Although we often feel self-conscious when talking honestly about what we want, we are usually worse about telling people, whom we otherwise like or depend on, about their limitations. We probably don't want them to return the favor and feel it's better to let each other live with our unspoken hopes and delusions. However, the failure to discuss expectations contributes more to the failure of close relationships than any other factor, whether these relationships are personal or professional. For example, in a romantic relationship, the man may enjoy the woman's company but fears that his continued attention will make her think that they will get married, leading him to withdraw. The woman, while in love with the man, is not ready to think about marriage; however, she may be worried about whether he's as attracted to her as she is to him. When he withdraws, it feeds her fears, and she begins to act more emotional than usual, which in turn affirms his worst fears. Consequently, what was otherwise the start of a beautiful relationship decays and frequently ends because the two people involved were too afraid to talk about their fear—the fear that the other person might have different expectations than they do, when probably neither of them really knew what they wanted.

The fact that the above example is so trite illustrates how pervasive this fear is in our personal relationships. What is probably less clear is how destructive this fear can be in professional relationships, particularly professional relationships where the parties have been close colleagues. People tend to form alliances when they have faced some mutual threat and cooperated successfully to counter it. During this process, they come to understand the other person's weaknesses as well as the strengths on which they depend. However, because they do depend on each other's strengths, they tend not to point out their weaknesses and overlook them instead. While many of us are aware of our weaknesses, if we could easily control them, they wouldn't be our weaknesses. The problem comes when your ally assumes that, as your business relationship progresses, you will support him in seeking some role or reward. But because the ally does not directly articulate what he expects and you don't want to risk disrupting what is working, you say nothing and wait. Usually you wait too long. Only under the pressure of some new challenge or risk do you risk asking your ally about his expectations, and you wind up handling the situation so badly that the relationship never recovers.

One of my early problems in management stemmed from the fact that I managed people the way I used to manage students. In part because I was so insecure about my own skills and thus not confident in criticizing others, I encouraged people to behave the way I wanted by focusing on what I thought their talents were rather than what I thought they needed to improve. In other words, I focused on how good they were and how much better they could be. When they failed to deliver, I acknowledged their shortcoming but didn't focus on my disappointment in them. Instead, I helped them recover their sense of confidence and pushed them on. The benefits to this approach were, for one, they liked my message, and for another, I avoided my own fear that they would become angry or disloyal to me. In the long run, however, this approach proved costly.

As I indicated earlier, at MCC we began the EXTRACT research project when my personal stock was down. Some said I was a bitch and a maniac and that no one with a brain would work for me. Although T, for whom at some level I had served as mentor, knew that characterization was not the whole truth, she chose to leave the project once we received funding, in part because she was tired of the sidekick position. Not wanting to leave me in the lurch, she waited until we had funding. Unfortunately, she waited until *just* after we had received funding and before I had had an opportunity to build trust with the sponsors. The funding had allowed us to hire a third person—F, whom we had both known at Texas Instruments—and T told me immediately after F accepted. (I found out later that she had informed F of her imminent departure prior to his acceptance, in case he wanted to change his mind.) I was extremely eager to fill T's position and push the project along before the research sponsors became nervous. They both suggested R, also from TI, as T's replacement. R checked out well so I hired her and bought another problem down the road because F and R failed to tell me that they were dating (which would have been fine had they not broken up about nine months later, a month before we needed to deliver our first demonstration). But that's another story. The point is that I was dependent on the skills

**155**

and commitment of two people I really didn't know and who were, at the time, significantly more loyal to each other than to me.

I managed F and R like students, praising them for the skills they had and minimizing their faults. We limped along and did moderately well, in part because of the core architecture of the design, their programming skills, and the fact that the problem we were solving was costly, complex, and as a result relatively easy to sell to research sponsors. (The fact that the price was relatively low helped as well.) I told F and R that we were going to start a company, and that idea appealed to them and helped add to the then larger group's camaraderie. As prominent contributors to the research project, they expected to be major players in the start-up. And I had done nothing to dispel these expectations because, operating through my fear of their revolting against me, I had never pointed out what I believed their limitations were. When the company was formed and they didn't get the prominent positions they felt they deserved, our relationship soured, and they rebelled—one by slacking off and the other by leading a revolution. Ultimately, I had to fire both of them. In both cases I had waited too long, had agonized too much, and did it badly.

The lesson here is how important it is to be frank with your allies throughout your relationship, especially when you sense that they think better of themselves than you do. You should not stop praising them for what they do well, but you need to balance that praise by telling them candidly what you think they need to work on. We often resist offering constructive criticism because we are afraid that the other person will get mad at us. Perhaps he'll even tell us something we don't want to hear about ourselves, but criticism rarely kills us. If we hear something negative about ourselves, either we will recognize it as true and face the option of trying to change our behavior and improve, or we won't agree and probably feel misjudged. Your allies have the same choices. If they don't agree with your assessment of their skills, they may argue with you or even get angry; however, few people will express their anger directly, in part because they probably recognize some grain of truth in what you have said. More likely they will feel less close to you, put more distance between you, perhaps leave the company, or in the worst case bear a grudge and lend some support to an enemy at a later time. While these reactions may not be pleasant, your honesty is significantly less costly than betrayal and the potential damage when they are surprised that they don't have your support.

## Conflicting Values

The best partnerships are based on mutual dependence, where each partner recognizes the strengths of the other and is brave enough to be open about where the other needs to improve. Although sometimes a personal chemistry can kickstart a good partnership, most partnerships develop in stages over time and establish some means for dealing with conflict. Note that this means of coping does not always mean quid pro quo or an even give and take. Sometimes one partner will never acknowledge being wrong but will internalize feedback he hears from the other. Other partnerships rely on a fairly even give and take. In these cases, the relationship can be so effective that it takes years for it to fail. Eventually it will fail, however, if at its heart the two people have sufficiently different value systems, because what a person values will determine how he defines success and how he copes with hardship and failure. For instance, if one partner cares more about having power while the other cares more about the quality of his personal life, each will react differently to success. If one partner cares more for external appearances while the most important thing to the other is to perform in accordance with her conscience, then their approaches to dealing with a venture-threatening condition may be very dissimilar. Sometimes, hard times help prolong a partnership, for as long as they confront worries about external threats or problems, they can avoid acknowledging what they don't like about each other. Afterward what leads to their parting are differences in what the two individuals believe constitutes happiness or success.

While mixed expectations often lead an alliance to an ugly end, the dissolution of many a good partnership is more akin to a divorce. It can be amicable or it can be full of pyrotechnics, but it is almost always accompanied by a sense of grief and failure—grief because after acknowledging the breech, each partner longs for many aspects of the "way it used to be" and failure because each blames himself for having trusted the other or having misled himself so badly. In either case, if they are lucky, they can manage the split in such a way that they retain respect and affection for each other.

## Impeding Trust

There is a long list of successful companies that were cofounded by two strong personalities. In technology these include Bill Gates and Paul Allen at Microsoft, Steve Jobs and Steve Wozniak at Apple Computer, and Bill Hewlett and Dave Packard at Hewlett-Packard. Yet as evidenced in the previous examples, often one of the seminal people chose to leave the company after it achieved success. Attributing these departures to the megalomania of the person remaining or writing them off to emerging value differences between partners may have an element of truth, but in this section I want to focus on another dynamic that I have witnessed that can also lead to the partnership's dissolution. Having two strong, often alter egos drive a start-up company often helps reduce risk and almost always brings comfort to early employees and investors. Hearing the same story from passionate people who share a vision and have complementary skills helps those outside the partnership believe that they are hearing the "straight story."

However, as the company grows and the complexity of the business increases, the bond between partners can serve as an impediment as more managers are added to the team. Like many entrepreneurs without significant management experience, at ETI I had an ideal of growing all our senior managers from within the company for several reasons. One came from the impression I had as a programmer at TI that part of why the company made such poor decisions was that too few managers knew or remembered very much about the work they were managing. (This sentiment led to the "Seventh of May" schools during the Cultural Revolution in Red China, where bureaucrats who had lost touch with the people's life were forced to work on farms or harvest fertilizer from public latrines in order to help them regain their values.) I also remembered feeling disturbed when Dell Computer went through a period when vice presidents were replaced on almost a weekly basis. The impression to the naive outsider was that of a banana republic with a different dictator every week. The other reason I favored promoting from within came from a feeling that it would help minimize politics and noise because the employees would know and presumably trust the individuals promoted to manage them, thereby eliminating the "what's he going to be like" speculation that follows hiring any manager from outside.

There are at least two reasons, however, why it is hard to achieve this ideal of developing management internally in a fast-growing company. The first is you will find so few people who want to step up to the emotional and moral requirements for being a manager (though many would like the title and the perks, as discussed in detail in chapter 7). The other reason that you bring in managers with experience is that managing large groups of people to accomplish a series of complex but interrelated tasks is more complicated than understanding how to perform one of those tasks effectively or than managing a team of six or seven people. As a result, in a fast-growing environment you frequently have to hire several outside managers in a twelve- to eighteen-month period to help drive the company forward. Accordingly, before people relax and feel comfortable again, you can't avoid some period of uncertainty.

While the dynamics between employees and a new and unknown manager are generally appreciated, the process for developing trust between the new manager and his fellow managers is not as well understood or appreciated. In large companies, quickly building the trust in and acceptance of new managers is not as important mainly because large companies have sufficient resources to afford a wider margin for error. They can hire managers, give them a set of goals, and judge their results. If the managers fail after the first twelve months, the company fires them and moves on. Smaller, high-growth companies face two impediments to taking this approach: The small company often cannot afford such a wide margin for error, and it can have a negative impact on morale.

A number of things appeal to people about working in a start-up company: the knowledge that their contributions are critical to the company's success, the sense of family—everyone knows each other, and even if they don't like some people as friends, they can appreciate their contribution—an understanding of every decision, and the sense of building something together. As a company grows, it is hard to maintain an environment that allows employees to feel this way. During this process founding managers face similar losses, going from the stage where they interview anyone to be hired to wondering if the person getting out of the elevator on their floor is a serviceperson for the copier or someone whose performance is critical to the company's survival.

There are studies about the different growth stages of companies and the various challenges they face at each stage. The transition from start-up to emerging growth is usually the stage at which companies need to hire outside managers. Another dynamic I don't think is as widely understood, however, is how integrating these new managers into an organization can be affected by the existence of two strong founding partners. Just as the employee wonders what the new manager is really like, the manager joining an emerging company wonders what his parameters are. He wants to know when his boss wants him to take the initiative and when he should take a more consultative approach. He also has to figure out how outspoken he can be with his boss, his peers, and so on. In the case of two strong founding partners, the new manager's questions are more complicated: "Do I have one boss or two? If I offend the number two person, will he disparage me to my boss? Can I criticize one partner to the other?"

If the bosses do not recognize these potential problems and send clear messages to the management team, a negative dynamic can occur where sympathetic managers talk to each other about what's really wrong and don't honestly confront their boss (or bosses). Then everyone loses, and the biggest loser is the company. If this situation persists long enough, the only way the CEO can demonstrate that he wants candid communication directly from all his managers and rebuild trust is to distance himself from his partner, thereby reducing the power of the relationship that was key to the company's early success. In fact, something similar happened to Robin and me.

As mentioned earlier, I benefited enormously from my partner and cofounder, Robin Curle. Particularly in the early days, when we were scrambling to make everything real—the product, the prospects, the company—it was so helpful to have someone with whom I could be totally honest and not fear reprisal or judgement. Because we were so close and trusted each other, I tended to accept Robin's assessment of what was going on and proceed from there. However, as she hired managers, problems arose. When they disagreed with other managers outside her organization, they would tell her their version of what was awry, and she would present their point of view to me. Because we were usually understaffed, pressed for time, and open to consensus-making, I would call all the affected managers into my office to discuss the issue rather than stage a series of discussions in which I could "discover" the problem on my own. This was a mistake. Rather than building a management team that resolved its own conflicts, I found myself feeling more and more like a schoolteacher in the sandbox telling the children how to get along. Even worse, some managers began to feel that if they didn't please Robin, she would have it in for them, and as a result, they were afraid to say anything that she might find critical. When I realized that we had landed in this situation, I felt bad for two reasons. First, I realized that I had failed as a manager. I should have spent more one-on-one time with all the managers, or, "Manage by walking around," so they would have known that I wanted their candid opinions. Second, to remedy the situation, I had to externally distance myself from Robin.

## What Is an Enemy's Value?

We have spent most of the chapter considering how to acquire and utilize allies and formulating reasons why alliances and partnerships fail. Before we leave the topic of personal relationships and how they pertain to warfare, we should discuss the concept of the enemy. First of all, it is important to recognize that there are two major kinds of enemies—those whose hostility is not personal but grows out of some situation where you are in conflict as to the desired outcome and those who are mortal enemies. For the latter you have come to represent something or someone that they will never forgive without some life-changing experience. You need to recognize the difference between the two enemies, because you should behave differently toward each.

With a sufficient number of negative experiences, you can turn almost anyone into a mortal enemy; however, for your own peace of mind, you should strive to have as few mortal enemies as possible. Admiral Bob Inman attributes his philosophy on the "conservation of enemies" to advice from Admiral

Rufus Taylor. Early in his career, Inman exhibited little patience for incompetence. After a meeting where he had been particularly outspoken, Admiral Taylor took him aside. When one becomes angry with someone else, he counseled, if it is a matter of principle, act immediately. Otherwise, let it pass. If it comes up again and there is a principle involved, act immediately; otherwise, let it pass. If the issue never involves the violation of a principle, it will eventually go away.

As a result, in the next chapter about going to war, we will talk about the importance of minimizing the personal enmity created by a conflict. If you fight well and you are fair, you will always have an opportunity to turn an enemy in one conflict into an ally in some other cause and often with a share of mutual respect. Your goal is to avoid going to war with mortal enemies, because with that intensity of feeling, you will not find a short road to peace. The battles will be costly and will end only when one of you is defeated and depleted.

You should also recognize that you can learn from your enemies. While negative feelings and energy are rarely productive, if you use the techniques we have discussed throughout this book, you can use your external enemies to help you identify your *internal* enemies and thereby reduce the number of external enemies you will feel the need to do battle with. In short, as you learn to control your inner demons, you learn to fear your external enemies less and to fight—like the adventurer—only when absolutely necessary.

# section III

# The Battle and Beyond

# Chapter 6

# Going to War
## Maximizing Your Chances for Victory

n earlier chapters we emphasized that habitual discomfort and irritation can signal the need for war and that frequently one would only be ready for war once the internal struggle is under control. In fact, internal struggles are key to spiritual development and should be encouraged. It is usually harder to decide to wage an external war because we frequently understand the significance of events only well after they happen.

> *One thing that makes art different from life is that in art things have a shape; they have beginnings, middles, endings. Whereas in life things just drift along. In life, somebody has a cold, and you treat it as insignificant, and suddenly they die. Or they have a heart attack, and you are sodden with grief until they recover to live for thirty petulant years, demanding you wait on them. . . . In life one almost never has the emotion appropriate to an event. Either you don't know the event is occurring or you don't know its significance. We celebrate births and weddings; we mourn deaths and divorces; yet what are we celebrating, what mourning? Rituals mark feelings, but feelings*

> *and events do not coincide. Feelings are large and spread*
> *over a lifetime. . . . Anyway, that is a thing that art does for*
> *us: it allows us to fix our emotions on events at the*
> *moment they occur, it permits a union of heart and mind*
> *and tongue and tear. Whereas in life, from moment to*
> *moment, one can't tell a piece of onion from a piece of dry*
> *toast.*[1]

As the quotation above suggests, life as experienced is not the same as life recounted. A man writing his autobiography will describe an escalating series of events that inextricably lead to his decision to behave in a particular fashion. And he will be accurate, but what he will not accurately record—in part, because they are harder to describe and less dramatic—are all the moments of self-doubt and false starts that led to his decision.

Even in the development of actual warfare, where the initial engagements might involve the destruction of lives and property, some period usually passes before the transgressed upon realize the aggressor's intent and level of malice. In business, where actions are less dramatic, emotions (usually) less intense, and often the opponents less introspective, you will recognize your need to go to war only after a considerable period of discomfort during which you have tried a variety of techniques to remedy the situation. In fact, one clue that I may need to go into "war analysis" is when I am confident that my opponent and I should agree on some basic points and we don't. If I become increasingly irritated over time and if I keep trying different ways of making her see the point but fail to make any progress, then I have a conflict to address with someone who does not share my goals or values. At that point I need to step back and rethink my assumptions about my opponent and, based on this analysis, determine how to proceed.

Since 1979, I have made several life-changing decisions—

the decision to divorce, the decision to change careers, the decision to start my own research project at MCC. In only one of these instances—the decision to change careers—do I remember consciously making the decision. The others I arrived at after a period of emotional discomfort during which I chafed against conditions that I ultimately couldn't live with. Although I was making more than three times what I had earned in 1980, in 1988 I was professionally miserable. After working an average of sixty hours a week for several years, I had been assigned to a project I didn't believe in, working in a program where I had no respect, and certain that I would be among the first to be laid off when the program failed. T and I had halfheartedly worked for a few weeks on trying to design a system on our own time. I dreaded the thought of finding another job and having to pretend that I wanted to be an outstanding employee when I was so cynical about how organizations worked.

When I first started on the proposal for the EXTRACT project, I didn't think about what it would take to get the project funded; I just wanted to capture our ideas about what needed to be done and why it was important. I knew that it would be hard to succeed because I was generally held in such low regard, but I behaved in such a way that my enemies had as little opportunity to attack as possible. I realized that ultimately I was at war for my professional survival and self-respect.

My point is that when we feel threatened, we rarely see the conflict clearly at the outset. More often, because we would prefer not to acknowledge feeling threatened, we focus on extrinsic issues that are not central to our fear, such as how political and hateful some manager is. But at some juncture the conflict becomes so strong that we have only one choice—fight or flee. And if you choose to fight, you are at war. If you go to war, you should fight to win. This chapter discusses important principles of warfare and how you can use them to maximize your chances for victory.

## Be Determined

With war comes risk and with risk comes loss. Even the most successfully waged wars entail some level of defeat or collateral damage. Therefore, if you decide to wage war, you must do so with the idea that no matter what happens, you will persevere until you are victorious or totally defeated. If you accept the possibility of defeat, you will find it. Remember, there are eight million ways to fail, but you only need to find one path to success.

It is important at the outset to understand the commitment you are undertaking in order to know the strength of purpose you must muster. In battling for some piece of internal turf within a large corporation, for example, the war may be over in a matter of months; however, depending on how you have conducted the battle, you may suffer in years of enmity. If, on the other hand, you are staging a revolution (perhaps a start-up), you may be taking on years of commitment. In short, don't go to war unless you are serious and committed to persevere.

## Be Dispassionate

Anger is a messenger, your subconscious's way of telling you that you are in danger. In the previous chapters, we have talked about how to analyze the fear behind your anger to understand how much risk actually exists. If a substantial part of the risk is external and you decide to go to war, you must will yourself to minimize the amount of anger you feel. Concentrating on your anger only reduces your ability to focus on what you need to do to achieve victory. That is not to say you must get over your anger. Instead, bank it like a fire so that you can rekindle it when you need it.

Fierceness in battle can be most effective. The Celts, who fought naked with their hair limed back and faces painted, intimidated the disciplined and armored Romans. Noting that the Celts treated birth with mourning and death with joy, Caesar cynically stated that this mindset accounted for their deeds of reckless bravery in battle. However, for most of us to be successful we must control our anger and use it as skillfully as any other weapon. Like a cat viewing its prey or like the martial artist, the most effective attack starts with a centered and focused state and usually with the minimum amount of effort. As military strategist Zhuge Liang of the third century C.E. maintained, "In ancient times, those who governed well did not arm, those who were armed well did not set up battle lines, those who set up battle lines well did not fight, those who fought well did not lose, those who lost well did not perish."[2] In short, anger must be replaced with logic and determination. As the old adage goes, Revenge is a dish best served cold.

I have had varying success remembering this principle in my own battle history. In general, I find it easiest to conquer my anger when I know expressing it will do me very little good, or when my situation is so dire that no one would care or be frightened by me. In these cases, I usually experience a sense of desperation and intense fear, as in the time when I was so miserable at MCC. Because the EXTRACT project was my last chance to avoid being forced into getting another programming job, I was determined not to repeat the mistakes I had made in the computer-aided design program. In every personal interaction and even with my friends, I reminded myself how badly many people thought of me, and I refrained from expressing anything negative too intensely or from speaking too critically of any particular individual.

Throughout the history of ETI my anger has also been my signal that at some level we are at risk. However, in part because I have been preoccupied with solving other material problems, I have been tempted to lash out—not intentionally at anyone, but out of irritation with the situation. Two things I have learned about running a company are sympathy with employers and that there are employees whose fate, for fear of being quoted, should go unspoken. For example, on three occasions we have discovered that one of our salespeople has been working for another company, taking base pay from both. On another occasion, a grudge between a supervisor and an employee—both high-maintenance women—finally resulted in an inappropriate altercation that ultimately led to one suing the other and the latter being counseled out of the company. In a small company where the welfare of all employees depends on the company's financial position, I can become fairly indignant when an employee fails to pull his weight; but I have learned to swallow my anger almost as soon as my adrenaline starts to flow, because expressing this fury only puts the company at risk. I have been less successful in addressing this anger when an individual's behavior (or that of an organization) is not in her own best interest. It makes me crazy when people won't cooperate with what will ultimately benefit both them and the organization. In these cases, I am tempted to make the mistake of expressing my frustration and showing my contempt. In these cases I failed to recognize that not everyone sees the world the way I do or puts the ultimate welfare of the company ahead of their individual success. These mistakes stem from my focusing more on my feelings than on the war's objective.

To be successful in warfare you must be dispassionate and even removed. If you have been adamant, acquiesce. If you have been hostile, appear contrite without actually apologizing. Strive to remain alert and observant, for only in this way will you be able to understand your enemy.

## Know the Enemy

By the time someone decides to go to war, she has a clear sense of the enemy. The problem is that it is *her* perception of the enemy, not the enemy's view of himself. However, if you are to anticipate the way the enemy will react, you must forget what you think about him and seek to understand what he thinks about himself. Frequently, when we believe that our principles are correct, we assume that anyone who disagrees with them is evil, as long-standing ethnic rivalries attest. However, few people relish being evil. Even sociopaths and psychopaths rationalize their behavior. As a result, you must assume that your enemy isn't evil, per se, but he just doesn't see the world the way you do. To determine the best strategy for defeating him, you should answer the following questions:

- What is important to him?

- What are his fears?

- How do you threaten him?

- How smart or talented is he?

## What Is Important to Him?

At the root of any conflict are differences in perception, frequently—but not always—resulting from a difference in values. Some have argued that there are four primary archetypes, each of which has a male and female side: the father/mother, the warrior/amazon, the adventurer/companion, and the sage/mediatrix. Each of these archetypes can be characterized by certain values they hold. The father/mother appreciates the respect earned for serving his/her role in the community and adheres to the values of the society; the warrior/amazon fights against evil and is very much rooted in the world; the adventurer/companion favors the personal and often unconventional path; and the sage/mediatrix builds a life around intellectual and spiritual exploration. You can see that there are some inherent conflicts among these archetypes. The warrior/amazon's life is rooted in action while the sage/mediatrix is rooted in contemplation, for example, while the father/mother's adherence to the community's principles may find the less conventional attitudes of the adventurer/companion threatening.

One could argue that while they share the warrior/amazon characteristics, entrepreneurs would more often be found among adventurer/companions and the CEO of a Fortune 1000-size company among father/mothers.

In assessing how to do battle, you should try to characterize the values that drive your opponent, determine how they differ from yours, and strategize how to minimize these differences. The ease with which you can prepare this way might depend on how recently you have had your values challenged. For instance, at MCC when my professional reputation had been seriously damaged, it was relatively easy to realize how the research scientist Dr. F and I differed. He had had an extremely successful career, first at a large company and then at MCC. Clearly he was extremely ambitious and considered himself superior to his supervisor. Given his success and its importance to him, as well as the vulnerability of my position, I knew openly opposing him would make him an enemy for life and for little purpose. My goal was not to obtain a senior-level position at MCC but to find a path to spinning out. Thus, even though Dr. F threatened my goal, I saw no benefit in thwarting his. In fact, because he was less than subtle—actually he was somewhat brutal—in how he dealt with anyone who crossed him, my best approach was nonviolent.

However, not long ago, I forgot my own advice. In 1996 a company I shall call X-Corp, one of the largest software companies in the world, approached ETI about becoming one of a handful of vendors to complete their "business intelligence" solution. After working with X-Corp for almost a year to perform due diligence and sign a reseller agreement, D, the X-Corp individual who had championed the relationship, retired for personal reasons. We were handed off to N, who had had very little involvement up to that point, was significantly less technical or aware of customer implementation issues than D had been, and was focused on the sale of the product for which he had been responsible for several years. For numerous years I had had significant input on ETI's business decisions regarding where we spent our resources, but I was not fully aware of the risk we were undertaking in this agreement.

Like many small company managers, I felt the joint business vision made sense. It never occurred to me that X-Corp would not follow through on its contractual obligations. I should have become suspicious when early on in the joint development X-Corp did not make certain resources available until I had called D regarding delays. But when D left, I lost all leverage. When I called N with similar requests, he always responded, "I have that problem, too." Foolishly, I focused on my irritation with him and the inefficiencies of the X-Corp organization rather than realizing the full extent of ETI's risk and how I was turning him into an enemy. To return to the archetypes, N was clearly a father/mother, his position in the establishment was more important than a particular adventure, or in this case the success of a particular market thrust. Given my bent toward the warrior/amazon, I didn't appreciate that his position—and more important, his power—within X-Corp was nothing to take lightly. My head-on, critical approach to what else needed to be done to sell and support the integrated solution more successfully threatened his goal of maintaining or improving his status within the hierarchy. Thus, N thought it was in his best interest to discredit the business potential of the joint solution, a tactic that was not entirely successful because their salespeople have sold so much of the product. Moreover, because most of the individuals who have reached the upper management of X-Corp believe—based on the company's sheer size—that they have little to learn, no one wanted to hear criticism of their approach.

If I had appreciated from the first that, despite the reseller agreement, our goals were different, I might have found a path around N. I still might not have been able to transform the relationship—we are not the only software vendors to have had such problems with X-Corp—but ETI certainly would have had fewer headaches. Because I was paying more attention to my irritation at N's failure to recognize how wrong he was, I forgot to think about what N found important and to modify my behavior to not (at least overtly) threaten his goals.

## What Are His Fears?

If you know what is important to someone, then you can anticipate what will make him uncomfortable. In N's case, for example, it was clearly important to look good in his new position and to validate the company's decision to promote him. Any situation that might lead to questioning his skill would make him uncomfortable. In any case, if at all possible, you should mount your campaign so that you do nothing to threaten your enemy overtly. Instead you should set the stage so that he reveals his shortcomings on his own or, better still, gets caught treating you unfairly. If, on the other hand, you consciously threaten your opponent, it is likely that the energy you must spend combating his hostility will adversely affect your ability to defeat him.

## How Do You Threaten Him?

Successfully avoiding overt hostility will be a function of whether you threaten your enemy, and if so, whether he is aware that he is threatened. Usually you would think that an enemy who is self-aware is more dangerous than one who is not; however, the opposite is often the case. Consider the example where you and your enemy are in competition for a promotion and your enemy believes you might have the edge. Depending on your enemy's values and temperament, he may choose to behave honorably and accept the potential for failure, or he may try to discredit you or get others to lobby on his behalf. The point is that his tactics, whether well-advised or not, have some logic to them. As a result, depending on your self-confidence and desire for the prize, you can also choose from a wide range of similar tactics.

Your situation is much more dangerous when the enemy is threatened but is unaware of his situation, because in this case, his reactions may not serve his own—or the company's—interests. For example, B, my boss at Texas Instruments, hated my style more than my content. My goal was to do whatever I could to deliver a quality product on schedule, exactly what would help him succeed as a manager; however, given his own fear of conflict and criticism, B found my confrontational (angry) style so distasteful that he refused to help me even when what I was demanding was in the company's best interests. While my hotheaded style no doubt exacerbated the problem, there is a good chance that even if I had taken a more measured tone, he would have had the same general reaction.

In short, it is doubly important to recognize when you threaten your enemy and he is not aware of it so that you minimize your contact and work around him. In fact, it was only after I realized that B didn't really care whether the product was released on time that I broke ranks and began to succeed. My earlier failure to step back from my feelings long enough to outwit him resulted in my wasting emotional energy and time and gave him even more ammunition for discrediting me with my colleagues.

### How Smart or Talented Is He?

Obviously, you must be careful of a smart enemy since she is more likely to outwit you or to lay a trap into which you could carelessly walk. If you are intelligent in your analysis of why you are willing to fight, it is likely that you can be a match for an equally skilled opponent. However, it doesn't follow that a less skilled or intelligent opponent is less dangerous. To paraphrase Jean Cocteau, never deal with an idiot, for if you do, you must deal with him on his level, and at that level, he is better than you will ever be. Of course, your enemy rarely is an idiot, but despite her failure to assess her skills accurately or to understand what is ultimately at risk, she may still be a formidable enemy and cost you many casualties.

For example, recall S, the woman I had mentored who became dissatisfied with her position in the company. Although she was bright and talented, she wasn't sufficiently skilled for the role she aspired to. While I told her my opinion early on and she appeared to agree intellectually, the underlying message was unacceptable to her. At an emotional level, S felt I had abandoned her for Robin, and as a result, Robin received things that S deserved: a higher position, more stock, and more visibility. S's shortcoming was that from her limited view of what was entailed in building a business, she could not appreciate that the skills Robin brought to the company were critical to the company's survival. However, S could relate to people emotionally and was in a key management position at the company. Moreover, she understood my weaknesses and used them to position me as a monster and Robin's "pawn" (her term) and herself as the employees' protector. As she garnered more and more support, she became more confident that her cause was just until she was brave enough to launch a revolution. Her defeat came because her view was so limited and her motive—to discredit me, the mentor who had (unfairly) judged her unworthy—personal. As a result, the Board backed me, in part, because they also valued Robin's experience.

But the damage caused the company was extremely costly. For months the entire development team—the group chartered with developing the products we sold—was in turmoil, resulting in a reduction in productivity of 50 to 60 percent, hardly an expense a company with revenues of $3 million could afford. Even more serious, we lost almost one quarter of the technical team. Some members were marginal, but others were extremely valuable, good people with good hearts and excellent skills, one of whom I had also mentored (which was probably why her loyalty was so important for S to acquire). Of those I most hated to lose, they left not because they bought S's story but because of their distaste for this kind of personal animosity that put the company in turmoil. Several went to work for a company, located in the next building, that subsequently shut down. I have often wondered what happened to them. Wherever they are, I am sure they are valued employees because they are wonderful people, and it grieves me that they may still think badly of me. But I won that war with S, and the company went on to prosper.

## The Enemy Is Not the War

We have spent a considerable amount of time in this chapter discussing ways you should think about the enemy, but do not let this level of attention lead you to believe that the goal of your war is to defeat the enemy. The enemy is the easy target. He thwarts and threatens you; you thwart and threaten him. But if defeating the enemy is your goal, you are too emotionally involved. While your enemy may have been the individual that helped provoke you to go to war, to focus on destroying him as your goal is like focusing on trying to eliminate evil. Evil—or in a more normal case, a serious, if not mortal, disagreement about perspective or values—will always be with us. Focusing on the enemy's faults and how to bring him to justice is not an ignoble goal, but it brings little value to the world. Rather, what we need from heroes is a model for how to transcend evil, how to be sufficiently effective in dealing with the enemy while focused on a higher goal.

If you are convinced that your company is on the path to failure and that individual X is aiding and abetting that failure, it is less important to defeat X than to help the company succeed. In short, even in the face of the enemy, you should strive to be dispassionate. This endeavor is not easy. I fail on a regular basis. But I have always found that success depends on transcending the personal and focusing on the outcome. In this way, the enemy becomes a rock in the road instead of your raison d'être.

## Embrace Uncertainty and Fear

The concept of self is relatively recent in the history of mankind. In *The Origins of Consciousness in the Breakdown of the Bicameral Mind*,[3] the psychologist Julian Jaynes argues that there is a physiological reason for why self-awareness is so recent. He maintains that people used to lack a sense of self because they interpreted the signals sent from the right side of the brain to the left side as external, something like the voices of gods. It was only when the two sides of the brain became more closely intertwined—roughly 3,000 years ago, according to Jaynes—that humans began to develop a sense of self and being.

One could argue that self-awareness is what differentiates humankind from other life forms, organic or electronic. The concepts of salvation and damnation are only possible if the individual recognizes his ability to control certain aspects of his thoughts and behavior. On the other hand, this very self-awareness is also the source of our greatest fear, because our awareness of what we can control is accompanied by an awareness of what we cannot control. This history of civilization can be seen as an attempt on the part of humankind to either control our environment, as in the case of science, or to rationalize how we should deal with not being able to control it, as in the case of religion. The goal of science is to understand, and the value of science is an increase in our power to control. Religion prescribes how man should behave to cope with his fears, thus enabling him to tolerate (or destroy) what he can't control.

Regardless of how individuals might balance the importance of science and religion in their own value systems, few would disagree that one of the things we fear most is uncertainty. Does he love me? Will the weather hold out for the harvest? Will she recover from cancer? Our inability to accurately predict outcomes not only gives credence to Marilyn French's claim that "in life, from moment to moment one can't tell a piece of onion from a piece of dry toast," but also accounts for why so few of us willingly go to war.

Great courage may be required to win a contest, such as a battle, an Olympic race, a boxing match, but even greater courage is required to recognize and embrace the commitment it takes to win a war or even to live a life that constantly demands that you strive for your personal best in the face of uncertainty. Consequently, when for whatever reason you are finally ready to embark on a professional war, you must accept uncertainty and use the fear you feel to keep you vigilant as you devise your strategy or execute your plans. That is not to say that you should focus on it. Energy spent worrying about an outcome is effort squandered. Worrying about whether your lover will want to marry you someday, whether your investments in the stock market will yield enough for a comfortable retirement, or if successful completion of your project will result in promotion does not help make any of those things happen. Assuming success is even riskier. While such techniques as visualizing success and neurolinguistic programming can help an individual psychologically prepare for success, wars are not won without facing conflict and gathering courage.

In short, you must embrace uncertainty and recognize that your strategy is not a roadmap but a set of assumptions and plans for how to respond should those assumptions prove true or false. When starting ETI, I did not know what it took to run a company. I was sure of only two things. First, if we could develop and support a product like ETI•EXTRACT, it would help companies save a great deal of time and money in their information technology organizations. Second, I knew how little I knew. For the first year, it was simply a matter of taking what appeared to be the next logical steps: looking for capital, finishing the product, and keeping expenses to a minimum, all while analyzing what went wrong whenever we got a negative response. Our attitude was that defeat was likely, but failure was unacceptable. It was our responsibility to face whatever setbacks we encountered and figure out how to get past them.

Almost every year has yielded another threat, as different but as frightening as the last. In the first year, we had to raise money. In the second year, we had to make the product work (we had not had the luxury of either the time or environment to test it properly before it went into the field). In the third year, we had to survive the revolution previously discussed. In the fourth and a good part of the fifth years, we had to complete the implementation of the next major release, which involved almost a total rewrite of the entire product. In the sixth year, our sales team was beginning to flounder. In the seventh year, we were still trying to remedy the sales problem and failing. In the eighth year, facing a second year of losses, we had to reduce our staff in order to cut expenses while trying to maintain the commitment and passion of those who remained. In the ninth year, we turned the corner and began to recover our momentum.

In the meantime, the company managed to grow from 50 to 70 percent from its second fiscal year through its sixth. Our products received AA ratings for three consecutive years from Crossroads, the annual conference conducted by Open Systems Advisers, which bases its awards on customer feedback. (We were the only company to date to receive this rating—their highest—for three consecutive years.) Our customers reported anywhere from a three-to-one to a forty-to-one savings over coding and maintaining their data interfaces by hand. Yet in spite of these signs of success, every year I find myself at some point lying in bed and wondering about whether we will survive or how to deal with an employee whose behavior was putting us all at risk. The uncertainty remains. Despite a huge market and a successful product, we may still fail because of management execution—and because I'm in charge of management, because of my execution. In short, uncertainty and fear are still my companions, and I still find myself licking my wounds, analyzing our predicament, and going out there again. The outcome? Stay tuned—news at eleven.

## Expect the Unexpected

Even the victorious can suffer defeat. Remember the Trojan horse. During the initial phases of war in the workplace, your enemies are obvious—doubts about your ability to deliver what you have promised, to keep the naysayers at bay, to ensure cashflow. To ensure against defeat in these areas, you work with your colleagues to establish processes and techniques, whether offensive or defensive. If you are talented, and lucky, you may succeed and believe that you have in place sufficient defenses to keep your forces whole. At this point you become vulnerable to the sneak attack or, in business, more likely the paradigm shift.

Success in warfare requires focus, concentration, and dedication. Unfortunately, sometimes the very energy that allows you to succeed against the initial threats can lead you to believe that by keeping vigilant in these areas you are safe. In reality, conditions change, sometimes because of your earlier success, and if you don't periodically step outside of the day-to-day fray to reexamine your assumptions, you run the risk of being defeated by some new opponent or condition that allows your enemy to leverage off the path you have paved.

Consider the U.S. car industry, for example. Invented in the United States, the U.S. automobile dominated the world market with its glory days in the 1950s and 1960s. The mass market belonged to the U.S. manufacturers, and they spent their efforts fighting each other for the biggest piece of the pie. In the meantime, the Japanese, recovering from their bitter defeat in World War II, reasoned that the U.S. public was tired of paying continually higher prices for cars of declining quality. By offering quality and performance, the Japanese took the U.S. market in the 1980s and surpassed the surprised U.S. car manufacturers.

On one level, it might seem easy to guard against the unexpected by simply questioning your assumptions on a daily basis. However, our ability to act effectively in the world is a function of our capacity to generalize, to filter out unimportant differences, and to focus on the few key factors that put us most at risk. In business and war, we accomplish this evaluation in part by learning to use others to serve as our filters. After all, no general wins a war single-handedly. We trust that our allies' judgment and behavior will be comparable to our own, and consequently we delegate large tasks to them with the expectation that they will consult us if there is any risk. Victory is a function of strategy and execution, and execution depends on the skill, commitment, and courage of others. Unfortunately, too often the unexpected comes from the people we have trusted and who have served us well. In such cases, the setback usually results from one of three sources: failure of heart, failure of skill, or failure of luck.

## Failure of Heart

You don't have to admire people to trust them. As long as you accurately assess their skills and values, you can plan around their shortcomings. For example, J is an employee who is consummately professional in his design and programming skills and can be counted on to deliver quality code on time or to give you the earliest notice when something unexpected is encountered. He is uncomfortable, however, when he perceives that other people are lacking. While he might see that the project is at risk because someone else is either not as skilled or not as committed as she should be, he is unwilling to confront the person directly or to rat on her. As a result, he may fail to alert you to an unexpected and unhappy surprise, but this misstep is not a failure of heart on his part. He is not trying to hurt you or the company; he is simply acting within the range of parameters in which he feels comfortable.

When someone you trust betrays you, it is from a failure of heart. This surprise can be the more bitter because you are tempted to spend too much time grieving and chewing on how you could have ever been so wrong as to trust the person in question. Like a spouse in a failed marriage, you then focus on all the faults you never saw and become angry at yourself as well as at the person who failed you. This behavior is not only counterproductive, it is shortsighted, because most often a person who betrays a trust is a person who feels that they have been betrayed. Mark Anthony joined forces with Cassius Longinus and assassinated Julius Caesar, for instance, because he was convinced that Caesar had betrayed the principles of the republic in order to glorify himself.

In my own case with S, the young woman who tried to lead an employee revolt, I felt wounded when she misjudged and mistreated me. Later I was able to see her point of view. She had been a talented and dedicated contributor. I had confided in her and depended on her commitment to perform. As my attentions turned from the product to the business, I shared less time and fewer confidences with her, in part because I didn't want her (or others) to know what a precarious financial position the company was in. Instead I spent more time with Robin, who was experienced in raising money and who served as my mentor.

I realized that S resented this change when I heard that she was calling me Robin's lackey. However, my own fear and insecurity regarding the company's survival prevented me from understanding that S's behavior grew out of jealousy, or her sense that I no longer appreciated her and that I had betrayed my commitment to her. And if you honestly remember when you felt jealous and peel back the anger you focused on the person who had replaced you in someone else's affections, you will remember how much it hurt to fear that you were somehow lacking.

To judge a person negatively for a failure in heart is to wallow in your own fear of littleness. It would be more valuable to focus on what series of events led the person who betrayed you to feel betrayed herself, and then to resolve that in the future you would find the courage to put your own fears and troubles aside and to spend time with those on whose loyalty you depend.

## Failure of Skill

Trusting a coworker requires that you feel comfortable that the person is well-intentioned, loyal, and has the skills required to be successful. The problem with warfare is that as the enemy becomes aware of his risk and mounts ever stronger campaigns to deter you, the difficulties and opposition tend to escalate before improving. During this period, an unexpected defeat can come from a failure in skill. When an assault comes from a comrade due to failure in heart, although he may not fully understand his motives, preferring to think of you as the devil incarnate, he does know his intentions. The trouble with a failure in skill is that the one who fails is usually unaware that he is failing, for if he could see that something in his behavior needed to change, odds are he would attempt to change it.

Your challenge in preventing this unexpected defeat is recognizing your comrade's limitations before extensive damage occurs. However, coming to this realization is hard for two reasons. First, because you trust the individual to successfully carry out the task assigned, he will have to fail before you are alerted that he has a problem. Next, because the individual does not recognize his own part in the failure, he will usually explain that some other person or factor is at fault. As a result, only after a series of failures will you suspect that the problem might be with the person to whom you have delegated the task. The difficulty you face at this point is telling this person, who has previously served you well, that you have judged him inadequate, for not only do you risk making an enemy, but you feel that you are being disloyal.

In my own case, I recognize two clues that alert me that I may be dealing with a failure in skill. The first is my own reaction to the person as the series of problems continue to mount.

If I find myself getting irritated with my comrade and impatient with his explanations, it is because I believe that he could be more effective and is just not trying hard enough. The second clue is when he does nothing to change his behavior despite the fact that we both agreed that his tactics must change. In other words, instead of stepping back and generating hypotheses about what he could do differently, he keeps doing the same thing only harder. At this point I have come to realize that it is probably the case that, according to the Peter Principle, the individual has gone as far as he can and must be replaced in order to maximize the company's chances of success.

At ETI, for example, we had a number of good and loyal managers who were effective as long as the number of people reporting to them was relatively small, but when they could no longer have direct contact with every task, they failed. Usually their failure stemmed from an inability to encourage leadership in subordinates. In one case manager G complained that although three of his employees were very talented technically, they were reluctant to manage or simply didn't have the people instincts to be promoted. After my continued insistence that G needed to delegate more or fail, he hired an older individual with some management experience who turned out to be all talk and no action. Finally, I confronted G with my judgment that he was failing, and he reluctantly resigned. G's successor subsequently trained the very same employees, who became excellent managers under him.

For the well-being of your team, as the person leading the war, you must recognize and act on failures in skill as quickly and dispassionately as possible, even if the you have to hurt the feelings of someone you value and who has been loyal and committed. (We will discuss this topic in greater detail in chapter 7.)

### Failure of Luck

Finally some defeats are not failures on the part of the heart or skill of the lieutenant you trust but are simply the luck of the draw. For instance, a competitor may come out with a superior product, or two key employees quit to form a start-up, or your lieutenant's wife or mother becomes ill, and he feels that his other responsibilities must take precedence. In other words, everyone has performed at their personal best, and you still lose. Well, that's the risk with war.

## Expect Casualties

We all want to avoid the pain of loss, even though it is part of the human condition. In warfare, however, you must expect to suffer the pain of loss, which comes in many forms—loss of friendship, loss of faith, loss of credibility, loss of money, loss of position in the marketplace, loss of innocence, loss of self-respect. Instead of dwelling on examples, I want to focus on the different types of pain these losses inflict because our ability to embrace and transcend that pain determines whether we will succeed at least in the spiritual, if not the material, world.

The psychologist Abraham Maslow maintains that humans are driven by a hierarchy of needs—(from lowest to highest) physiological, safety, social, esteem, and self-actualization—and that we only seek satisfaction of a higher-level need when our lower-level needs are met.[4] In other words, someone who is hungry or homeless first will focus on fulfilling his physiological or safety needs rather than on finding intellectually stimulating work. Maslow's concept is useful in characterizing the two major kinds of losses you experience in warfare—the real and the symbolic. Real losses are those that affect our ability to satisfy the needs at the bottom of Maslow's hierarchy. If you go to war at work and execute badly, you may lose your job. If you start a company, it may fail, and you and your employees will be out of a job. In part because the results of these failures are so concrete, it is relatively easy to know how to address them.

Needs at the hierarchy's higher level are likely to be more

personal, with less agreement between individuals about what's important. Thus, how we should respond to them is often less apparent, particularly in the context of war in the workplace. For example, a sense of autonomy is extremely important to my self-esteem. At one level, of course, few, if any of us, are completely autonomous unless we choose to live as survivalists in the wilds, and even then we are dependent on the environment. For me, being autonomous is when I can use my own judgment to dictate my behavior rather than having someone else dictate how I should behave or what I should believe. I am sure that my feelings in large part result from the fact that I was raised in a house where my father insisted he was always right, and we were terrified of crossing him. Countless times he would say to me, "Change your attitude," which to me was even more oppressive than if he had told me not to do something. (Actually until I graduated from high school, practically all I did was study so maybe the only thing he could correct was my attitude.)

I have often wondered if part of the reason I started a business and gravitated to the position of CEO was to help enforce my illusion of autonomy. On the one hand, when you're the boss, very few people give you orders about how to behave. On the other hand, while a CEO is in position to make and be responsible for judgment calls, she is probably answerable to more constituencies than any other employee in the company. CEOs are responsible to the investors, the board, the customers, and the employees; and although they may (even correctly) blame a particular failure on someone who works for them, they are accountable—and ultimately vulnerable—if too many mistakes are made. One of the losses I have felt over the past two years, in fact, is the loss of that sense of autonomy that my role initially appeared to provide.

In the spring of 1997, ETI had to face some hard truths about its viability in making an initial public offering. While the company had experienced excellent growth from 1992 through

1997, we realized that we were not going to be able to sustain this kind of performance. Not only had we stinted on putting in the kind of information technology systems we needed to efficiently run our organization, but we encountered a serious problem with a piece of embedded software we had licensed to use in our new product release. Fixing both of these problems was going to require time and money. But even more important, our sales projections were far from what we had expected, we were eight salespeople short of our plan, and the productivity of the sales force in North America was slipping. We pulled the offering, ate a couple of hundred thousand dollars in costs, and then went about fixing what was broken, which took two years and most all of our discretionary cash.

I experienced innumerable losses during this period—sleep, money, trust, respect—but probably the most painful was the loss of my illusion of autonomy. People whom I respect have pointed out that I have too much guilt about the mistakes I made in running ETI and that my need to beat on myself may have hampered the company's ability to recover. These observations are probably true, but I have discovered that what I had consciously thought was my path to professional and financial autonomy meant I had subconsciously taken on a huge burden of responsibilities. In other words, instead of feeling freer, I felt more bound and with each subsequent shortcoming more guilty. Even though the company appears to have turned around, I find myself questioning my definition of what I need to feel satisfied with my own performance and what this may require in terms of how I behave. In conclusion, one of the casualties you encounter in war may be your peace of mind.

## Reassess Your Goals Regularly

War isn't for sissies. It requires courage, determination, and discipline, and it always brings pain. As a result, it should be undertaken only as a last result and continued only if the costs incurred are not cumulatively greater than the benefits afforded by victory. Fortunately, war in the workplace is rarely a matter of life and death; few of the readers of this book are struggling to meet their needs at the lower levels of Maslow's hierarchy. You can change your mind and withdraw without fear of a firing squad. If you have been struggling for a long time without achieving victory, it may be best for everyone concerned for you to declare defeat—or not. That is a judgment that only you and your conscience can make.

## Notes

1. Marilyn French, *The Women's Room* (Wayne, N.J.: Ballantine Books, 1988).

2. Thomas Cleary in the translator's introduction to San Tzu's *The Art of War* (Boston: Shambala, 1988), p. 9.

3. Julian Jaynes, *The Origins of Concsiousness in the Breakdown of the Bicameral Mind* (Boston: Houghton Mifflin, 1977).

4. Abraham Maslow, *Motivation and Personality* (New York: Harper, 1954).

# Chapter 7

# Learning to Lead
## Why We Love and Fear Authority

Heroism and power are not unrelated, but they inspire distinctly different reactions in people. Courage is the defining characteristic of the hero; its power allows the hero to defend her convictions in the face of risk. Most of us admire courage and fantasize about situations where we exhibit the hero's courage and skill. Power is another thing altogether. Power refers to one's ability to affect the fate of others. As a result, most of us feel ambivalent about people in power, because their power presents a potential risk to our well-being. We worry that our boss or governor or president doesn't value or care enough about our situation. On the one hand, we hope that he will be the good father figure who appreciates and looks out for us, and on the other hand, we fear either that he is not the exemplary person we hope him to be or that he does not respect us.

Thus far, we have discussed techniques for recognizing and analyzing when fear is driving us to warfare. One of the fears that we have not discussed is the fear of one's own strength and leadership capabilities. If you feel strongly enough to take on warfare in the workplace, your very willingness to face risk—or your courage—may thrust you into the role of leader, and you may have great ambivalence about accepting this role. In this chapter we will explore what people fear and want most in a leader, as well as why so many people are hesitant about both assuming and relinquishing a leadership position.

## The Distinction between Leader and Manager

It is important to distinguish between the terms *leader* and *manager*. If asked to choose which are more important, skills in leadership or skills in management, most of us would immediately say skills in leadership. Yet we should not diminish the importance of being a good manager. These skills are as important to a leader as was the medieval warlord's ability to bear a sword. We may underestimate the importance of good management because either we have never done it or in our experience the people promoted to management positions are so poor at it. In either case, part of our problem is perspective. Just as it is hard for someone engaged in hand-to-hand combat to understand why losing one particular battle is less important than establishing the ability to fight on another front, it is often hard for us to understand the perspective of those in power.

When I was working at Texas Instruments, I was asked to write a status report for the president of the Data Systems Group. I crafted what I thought was an excellent three-page report only to have my boss hand it back to me, telling me it was too long and that anything going to that executive level should be no more than a page. I remember thinking, What's the matter, can't these big shot executives *read*? I didn't understand then that I was suffering from a limited perspective. As part of my motivation to work the sixty-hour weeks required to make the delivery dates, I was convinced that my project was of key importance to the company and that the president would want to have detailed knowledge of its status. I still don't think my attitude was a particularly bad one. At ETI, I want everyone to think that what they are doing is of key importance to the company: otherwise, they will not give it their best efforts, and the company will suffer.

What I didn't appreciate then, when I was part of a six-person team, and what I do appreciate now that I am responsible for over 150 employees working in six countries is that at a certain point a manager can't know everything that is going on because of the magnitude of the operation. In the early days, I used to read and track every problem report with the software; in fact, because at the time I knew the code, I would sometimes send the support people a suggestion for a better way to answer a question. Likewise, I read every status report sent in by one of our consultants in the field, because these data points helped me understand both how solid the product was and how well we were setting expectations and providing service to the customers. However, finally I could no longer do this reading in addition to the rest of my job because the sheer volume of information was overwhelming. (In the days of the Internet, I think information overload is better understood than when I was toiling away as a lowly programmer at TI.) If I was going to raise money, monitor pesky partners like X-Corp, or deal with process, personnel, and infrastructure issues, I needed to delegate someone else to monitor the details of our progress in development, customer satisfaction, and collection issues and to let me know—at a much less detailed but accurate level—what the company was doing.

At the same time, the employee who is engaged in a particular project needs to understand why the company is taking some particular action. For example, one of the challenges ETI faced in the early years was shifting the product developer's priorities based on any number of factors: for example, a big deal where the customer would buy only if we agreed to provide a certain type of functionality by a particular date, some problem with the software that was keeping a customer from getting their project completed, or a shortage of consultants in handling the training and initial set-up for new customers (a happy problem). We were constantly asking programmers to stop what they were doing for a while and solve another problem and then go back to the initial project without losing any momentum. They were extremely frustrated because good software engineers are perfectionists and want to be given enough time to ensure that their work is complete. By telling them why the shift in priorities was critical to the company and assuring them that we would work to avoid similar situations in the future, we kept the spirit of the team going.

Managers face an even harder task when the company must take some difficult action, such as a staff reduction, a reorganization, or the termination of a popular employee. In this case, they must be ready to address their employees' more complex emotional reactions or run the risk of low morale and the reduced productivity it brings. Here the managers must decide how much they can say. In today's litigious culture saying anything negative about any ex-employee is dangerous, even if the company has evidence of incompetence or wrongdoing. The successful manager is able to articulate the trade-offs from a corporate standpoint, that is, that the decision can be justified in terms of what benefits the greatest number of people involved.

In case you are tempted at this point to go into a riff about management's focus on profits at the expense of the workers, review the material in chapters 1 and 2. In today's global economy, revenue growth and profitability are tied to a company's ability to raise the money it needs to do business. That is not to say that executive management always makes good decisions, however. Sometimes, just as in the lower echelons, important information is not visible from its perspective. I recently found myself expressing the same criticism of X-Corp's management for failing to make the right investments in the training and packaging required for our joint venture to achieve its potential. The problem there is twofold: The manager who owns our relationship neither understands the market (once again, per-spective—he is too far removed from the customer) nor wants to champion the relationship (remember, he inherited it from an individual who retired for personal reasons). Also, a $20 million revenue stream just isn't big enough to get a CEO's attention when he is dealing daily with figures in the hundreds of millions or billions.

Being a good manager is a demanding job. You must excel at analysis to track the progress of multiple people assigned to multiple tasks and to help determine the best set of trade-offs when something unexpected happens—and it always does. You must make the right judgment calls about how much detail to present to your manager, peers, and subordinates in order to keep them apprised of your organization's progress and to ask them for input when some cross-functional cooperation is required. You cannot be afraid of conflict; you must be able to say hard things directly but fairly, whether it's to an employee regarding his performance or (more difficult) behavior, a peer regarding some problem in delivering on their commitments, or even your boss if you think she has made a bad judgment call. Likewise, you must be able to encourage people to grow in their interpersonal and professional skills. Finally, you must understand how to honestly and accurately present the company's decisions and priorities in a way that addresses the concerns of the people who report to you, while inspiring their loyalty and commitment. Note that you cannot effectively achieve this last goal unless you are yourself either at peace with the company's decisions or a consummate actor or actress.

With this list of job requirements, it is not surprising that there are as few people who excel at management as there are who excel at parenthood. Most of us who take on either job fall short of our goals.

What distinguishes leaders from good managers is that they not only have a good mix of management skills, but the ability to win the hearts and minds of the people they lead so that they have faith that the correct values are in place even if they are not privy to the details. A leader's talents not only include an understanding of the skills of the people they manage, but a talent for empathy and storytelling. The talent for empathy is obvious; understanding what people feel is key to helping convince and motivate them. The prerequisite for storytelling is less obvious, because in today's cynical atmosphere, people tend to portray the storyteller as someone who distorts the truth as opposed to someone who distills it. However, in the early medieval times, the poet—or "shaper" (*scop*) in Old English terminology—held one of the most highly respected positions in society. And of the outstanding leaders of the twentieth century, such people as Winston Churchill, John F. Kennedy, Martin Luther King, and Nelson Mandela drew much of their power from their skills as orators. Ultimately, we all want leaders as well as dogma to help us focus our talents and passions in a world that can be both confusing and cruel.

## What People Fear or Want Most in a Leader

Having a strong leader can be comforting. If we are under the guidance and protection of someone powerful whom we also respect, it can significantly reduce the amount of anxiety we feel about the aspects of our life that we cannot directly control. And yet the very things we look for in a leader—power, authority, responsibility, and courage—also make us somewhat afraid of that person. In this section, we consider what makes us ambivalent about the people who exhibit these qualities.

### Power

People obey a leader they fear but follow a leader they trust and respect. In both cases, the individual in question has power. The big difference between them is in how that individual values power and how he obtained it. In a dictatorship or authoritarian culture, those who do not cooperate face dire consequences, and thus those with power have an added edge. In more liberal environments, people whose primary goal is to seek power or advancement in a hierarchy may be good managers or good people, but they use their skills in accordance with their own goals of achieving power. Sometimes these individuals are effective leaders, for example, in the case where they are aligned with ethical and effective organizations. Too often, however, they are not, and as a result most of us both respect and fear power. We want our leaders to be powerful, but we also fear that their desire to retain power at any cost may cause them to ignore our interests or the best interests of the company as a whole.

Leaders may value power but only to the extent that it helps them achieve their goals. They may be as insensitive to the needs of the people they lead as someone who is hierarchy-driven, but people consider them more trustworthy because their behavior is more likely to put their power at risk. Because leaders do not value power for its own sake, they are often willing to take risks and oppose those higher in the hierarchy to advance their case. As a result, they gain power in the eyes of the people they represent through these successful encounters with the power structure, whether the battle was one of driving a project plan through a large organization or successfully getting funding for some start-up venture. For example, consider the power of Martin Luther King or Cesar Chávez. Much of their power came from their willingness to repeatedly put themselves at risk while maintaining their principles. As they persisted in pursuing their goals in spite of hostility and overwhelming odds, they gained the respect of greater and greater numbers of people.

### Authority
Authority is the assumption of power, that is, the assumption that you have the right to the power you have obtained and that it is acceptable for you to act on it. In most cases, it is easier

for a potential leader to accept that she has power than for her to assume the authority that goes with it, because when a leader assumes the mantle of authority, she takes on not just responsibility, but the right to determine and judge. Judgment carries a strong emotional weight for most of us. Most of us are highly self-critical and, whether we admit it or not, keenly aware of our limitations and "unworthiness." Likewise, most of us are as critical or even more so of others, mentally noting that while Lucy may be a charming hostess, she has marginal taste, or that Robert can't bear to be wrong and as a result winds up arguing the most ridiculous positions.

Yet while we may be merciless in making these judgments in our own minds, few of us are comfortable or effective in making them public unless we do so in the context of some group quivering with self-righteousness. The Inquisition and McCarthyism were movements fueled by the need to damn others. On a less grand scale, occasionally there's a hothead in the workplace who rails about one or more of his coworkers or bosses (I've done this on one or ten occasions), but these open and vocal judgments tend to make others uncomfortable. Outside the protection of a group that endorses hatred, most people would rather make equally damning or even more vitriolic assessments only in the safety of their small trusted groups, whether colleagues at the office or their supportive audiences at home.

Part of what we want and expect in a leader is someone who will make and articulate those hard judgment calls so that we can see justice done without personally having to articulate them ourselves. However, we always run the risk that one of the hard judgment calls the leader may make will be directed at us, so a sense of anxiety accompanies our relief when we see our leader assuming the prerogative of authority.

## Responsibility

We all have responsibilities and are honor-bound to meet them. However, most of us enumerate our responsibilities in terms of what we personally should do, whether it's meeting a deadline at work, tithing at church, or helping our children with their homework. If we feel responsible for our children's well-being, we tend to measure it in terms of our ability to do such things as be consistent with discipline, provide them with braces and tuition, and set a good role model. While we expect our leaders to be responsible for the welfare of the people they lead, they are not personally responsible for performing the required tasks. Instead leaders are responsible for assuming the authority to decide what should constitute the group's priorities and to ensure that each individual in the group performs his or her assigned tasks adequately. The more we can feel comfortable that our leaders have accepted this responsibility, the more we can relax about the group's potential for success. However, no war is won on the strength of the general's commitment alone. We must also believe that all those upon whom the leaders depend feel equally responsible, and we worry that if the leaders shoulder too much of the blame when things go wrong, they will not demand from others the performance required to succeed.

## Courage
Probably the most important attribute we want from a leader is the courage to act for the group's benefit with minimum regard for his own well-being and self-interest. Whether it's a matter of being more outspoken with upper management at the risk of termination, or reducing staff when revenues have fallen off, or facing the dragon in his lair, we want our leader to be willing to do what we are afraid to. In extreme cases, as with Mohandas Ghandi or Anwar Sadat, this courage can lead to martyrdom. While we know this level of courage is critical to a leader's ability to succeed, we are often uncomfortable with it, both because we worry about summoning our own courage to follow and because we fear we may be victims of some collateral damage should the leader fail.

## Why People Are Hesitant to Become Leaders

Most of us would rather be appointed a position of power than actively seek the position, usually because we worry more about our virtues than acknowledge them. For example, we may have doubts that we are as smart as other people seem to think we are, or as pure of heart, or as committed. Even those who are most ambitious or political seek to have power and authority conferred on them rather than assuming it, if only to have external validation of their skills and promise. On the one hand, this tendency can be seen as modesty, but on another it is a form of cowardice. If you take on a position of power and authority at someone else's behest, whether that of a corporation or a group of people, then if you fail, you can say to yourself that you were never sure that you could pull it off, but you did your best. On the other hand, you may fear that if you volunteer for the role of leader and subsequently fail, others will think you are guilty of failure *and* arrogance.

However, at some level this reluctance to take on the power and responsibility commensurate with your talents is counterproductive in your dealings with others and a means of avoiding personal growth. Raised in the South before Betty Friedan and the feminist movement, I was taught that certain behavior was unfeminine and undesirable. As a result, like many women I became skilled in the art of manipulation. While it would be unseemly to tell a man that his idea was bad, it was perfectly acceptable to innocently ask a series of questions that would lead him to this conclusion. In fact, I carried this rather annoying trait well into my graduate school career, where I would preface a correct answer with something like "This may be all wrong, but. . . ." And yet throughout that period, the people around me considered me extremely smart. Consequently, my behavior was seen as disingenuous and actually prevented me from developing meaningful relationships with my peers. Even more important, my setting up so many false barriers kept me from facing challenges that would have led to personal growth. As a result, I only faced these hurdles later in life, when my situation was so desperate that I couldn't afford to play my own games.

Of course, having the courage to acknowledge your talents and power can help you rise to the role of leader, but it is typically not the driving force. Frequently, courage is kindled when your conviction or anger about some situation becomes so strong that you are willing to run the risk of failure and of losing the support of the very people you are depending on to help you succeed. Ironically, when people sense this level of resolve, they are most willing to follow. Of course, they have to believe that the war is being waged for the greater good and that you have the skills and commitment to be in charge. What finally makes them willing to support you, however, is their sense that you will make and stand by any hard judgment call required, regardless of the cost. In the following section, we will examine some of the difficult tasks a leader faces as well as guidelines that could help you in these situations.

## Why It's Hard to Lead

As discussed above, many people who lead do so as an extension of their commitment to a principle or values rather than from a desire to be important or exert power over others. One of my favorite books is *Njal's Saga*, the greatest of the Icelandic family sagas.[1] Written in the thirteenth century about events that took place 300 years before, this book—much like Truman Capote's *In Cold Blood*—is a fictional retelling of a set of historical incidents. In the case of *Njal's Saga*, it is the tale of two lifelong friends—Njal, the greatest lawyer in all of Iceland, and Gunnar, the greatest warrior. Much like what happens in a Western movie, Gunnar's skill and integrity attract animosity and challenge, and he is drawn into a series of confrontations that will ultimately result in his death. As he successfully fends off one attack after another, the intensity of the assaults increases until he finally kills someone. Afterward Gunnar asked his brother, "But I wish I knew . . . whether I am any the less manly than other men, for being so much more reluctant to kill than other men are."[2] Of course, what bothered Gunnar was that he didn't want to fight, but his honor—and his life— depended on defending himself well when attacked. Many people who wind up in leadership roles are analogous. They don't set out to assume authority and in fact are reluctant to do so, but they are driven to leadership when confronted with a situation they find intolerable. In this section, we discuss the fears people have about assuming leadership as well as techniques for overcoming them.

In general, these fears are related to what people want and fear most in a leader. While power, authority, responsibility, and courage are all key to helping someone successfully lead, these attributes also allow the leader to be less dependent on his followers, thereby putting at least some of them at risk. Likewise, the person assuming leadership, whose success is contingent upon her followers' support, fears that in performing the role required of the leader she may lose their support.

## The Interdependence between Leaders and Followers

Leaders know that their success hinges on the loyalty and performance of the people they lead. As a result, most new leaders are hesitant to anger or hurt anyone who works for them. They prefer to lead by example and praise rather than directly criticize someone. This approach can work effectively in small groups when the skills required of the leader are not significantly different from those of her people and when both parties have strong mutual respect. In fact, this arrangement was in good part the basis for the *comitatus* tradition that served the medieval Germanic world so well.

In *Germania*, the first-century Roman historian Tacitus describes the comitatus in the following way:

> Both prestige and power depend on being continually attended by a large train of picked young warriors, which is a distinction in peace and a protection in war. And it is not only in a chief's own nation that the superior number and quality of his retainers bring him glory and renown. Neighboring states honor them also, courting them with embassies and complimenting them with presents. Very often the mere reputation of such men will virtually decide the issue of war.
>
> On the field of battle it is a disgrace to a chief to be surpassed in courage by his followers, and to the followers not to be equal to the courage of their chief. And to leave a battle alive after their chief has fallen means a life of infamy and shame. To defend him and protect him, and to let him get the credit for their own acts of heroism, are the most solemn obligations of their allegiance. The chief fights for victory, the followers for their chief.[3]

The main "distinguishing characteristic of the *comitatus*" is "its reciprocity—more precisely, its being at once vertical and reciprocal . . . [O]nly the *comitatus* combined both qualities and made the assumption that the leader in a vertical relationship had obligations as much as did the follower and that therefore a voluntary element existed on both sides."[4]

This model of leadership seems particularly appropriate to today's professional worker who views himself as a free agent. It is also appealing because it emphasizes values most of us admire—an appreciation of interdependence and the importance of loyalty as opposed to the importance of power. While this model remains an ideal, it becomes somewhat harder to obtain in larger organizations, where the roles of the leader and the followers are more differentiated and perhaps they find it harder to appreciate each other's skills. When five or ten people are clearing a field or working on a tight deadline on a software project, each can easily recognize who is doing what and the value the coworkers bring to the team. When the team grows to twenty or thirty and is working in a company of 200 or 2,000 other employees, it becomes impossible for any one person to have a grasp of the effectiveness of all but a small group of others.

As a result, as discussed in chapter 3, the most important thing a leader can do is to take the time to explain, not just the goals of the group, but the issues facing the company and the trade-offs she must make. While everyone benefits from a good public relations person, in these less heroic times, the leader must serve as her own historian, not to self-aggrandize, but to share her reasoning. That said, the leader usually has to confront several hard decisions that she cannot share with her employees, either because they should not be made public (for example, the critical assessment of an employee's performance and potential) or because they can only be made public after the fact (for example, a staff reduction). In the following sections, let's consider the fears every leader must conquer.

### Fear of Judging

In part because we want the people we serve to like and respect us, we often find it hard to be direct and criticize their performance or skills. However, a leader or good manager must make these judgments and voice them, fairly and accurately, to the person being judged. If you are an inexperienced leader, you may avoid criticizing those who are not performing and focus your time on people you believe are performing well. Yet this behavior makes the situation even worse with the nonperformer. If you fail to address one employee's shortcomings, you are diminished in the other employees' eyes because you have abdicated your authority by not fulfilling the responsibilities of a manger. Worse still, the nonperforming employee may develop a higher opinion of herself than is warranted so that when you are finally forced to be honest, it comes as a terrible blow.

There are several things that can help you deal with these discussions, although some of them you will have to implement over time. First, although you may want the people you lead to like you, you must not need their approval or you will not succeed in fulfilling your role. Next, as we will discuss in the Letting Go section below, you must expect that at some point whatever respect and affection you have earned will diminish, as that is the natural order of things. Then if you care deeply for the people you lead and want them to feel happy and productive you must help them accurately face their strengths and weaknesses and give them an opportunity to outgrow their limitations. Otherwise, you have indeed judged them. Finally, you must also feel comfortable being criticized and recognize that you don't have to be perfect, even if you have assumed the authority and responsibility of serving as a leader.

## Fear of Violating Trust

Over time, then, you can approach critical assessments of yourself and others with sufficient detachment to actually see it as a form of problem solving. Once you have acquired this skill and served as the shaper of the group's history, leading can put you in a difficult position when you feel that you cannot be honest with the people you lead. These situations often involve trade-offs that could or do adversely affect valued members of the group, but if you speak about them before the fact—and violate your manager's trust—the group members' reactions could lead to an even worse result.

For example, consider the case where a company is losing money in a particular division, let's say, a software division of a hardware manufacturer. Management may decide that the problem is not with the product, that the company doesn't have enough critical mass in software to justify having a specialized sales and support group, and that the best thing would be to sell the division off to a software company working with the same customer base. If a leader privy to this information shares it with his people and the word gets out, a number of the division's best people—technical as well as sales and support—will probably seek employment elsewhere, thereby further driving down the company's revenues. Thus, the revenues of the division will probably fall, the company will be less likely to get a reasonable return on the sale (if it can sell the division at all), and more people will be adversely affected. When a leader is usually honest with his people, keeping this information private feels like a terrible betrayal of his values; however, to the extent that the leader is accountable—either wholly or in part—for the well-being of the entire organization, withholding this kind of information is one of his responsibilities.

### Fear of the Courage Required

Perhaps the leader's most important burden is her commitment to persevere in the face of adversity. All wars entail defeat and loss. If there is no risk of failure, it's not a war. The leader must fulfill his obligation and remain resolved, even if he begins to lose favor with the people he leads. In short, it's not important whether folks are making fun of you in the coffee room. If you lose your resolve, the war is over and you have lost. There have been times in the history of ETI when I have been extremely unpopular. I suffered many sleepless nights and sore jaws on many a morning from clenching my teeth, and while I confided in a few close friends, I had to remain firmly resolved in front of the employees.

Assuming the responsibilities of a leader entails learning to do hard things and keeping a good part of your feelings to yourself so it's little wonder that many extremely talented people hesitate to take on the role. If they do, they may well lose the affection and respect of the people whom they care for and respect. As a result, many people take on leadership positions only when they feel that they have no other choice. Either the company is in such a tight position that if they don't help, they will be failing their colleagues, or they are more convinced of their own ability to follow through than that of anyone else. (Note that making this choice does not mean that they think they are the most talented people. I once heard Ann Richards say to a senior executive of a $16 billion firm, "I wasn't the best person to serve as governor of Texas; I was just the best one running.") In my case, I couldn't do anything else for a living that I would feel comfortable about since I felt there was no point in working in business unless I could bring value to the marketplace. (Perhaps the company would have been better off if my goal had been to get stinking rich.)

In conclusion, one of the hardest conflicts most leaders face is that between the values of the comitatus tradition and the trade-offs of dealing with larger, more complex organizations. In the June 1999 *Fortune* cover story "Why CEOs Fail," the authors cited "people problems" as one of the top three reasons for failing, along with "lifer syndrome" and "bad earnings news." Even the toughest of the tough reported that dealing with people issues was one of their hardest problems. While we would like to think that business, as opposed to art, academia, or government, is objective, the ultimate "gating" factor is the human soul—theirs, ours, and that of others.

## Letting Go

While many people find it hard to assume the role of leader, once they have, it is often harder to let go—either of the level of their day-to-day involvement or of the role of leader altogether—even though the success of the war may depend on it. In this section, we will focus on why it is often tough for a strong leader to let others lead and on how to recognize when the time has come to relinquish the role of leader altogether.

### Identifying Leaders

It is often said that entrepreneurs are good at starting things but not at running them. Likewise, many leaders who are effective in small groups do not remain effective as the organization grows because they do not appreciate the importance of having equally strong leaders under them. When the first-time leader who values solidarity looks for lieutenants, he too often looks for people who are like him and would be loyal to him. From the comitatus ideal, this instinct would seem well-founded, because so much of the group's success in warfare depends on loyalty between members of the group. However, in today's more technically complex and specialized world, using these guidelines to choose lieutenants proves ill-advised in the end, because you will hire or promote people who have your same limitations instead of people with complementary skills and expertise who can increase the group's chance of success.

I personally made this mistake at ETI in hiring my first round of managers from the outside. I had always personally favored the notion of promoting from within, thinking that managers who came from the people they managed would have already proved themselves in the company culture and won the respect of their colleagues. While some of my best managers have successfully built their teams this way and helped develop some leaders under them, during the first five years of the company we were growing too fast to follow this approach. We couldn't afford to let someone learn how to create a profitable consulting organization; we needed someone who already had those skills. Similarly, our financials required someone who had a breadth of finance and accounting experience. We found headhunting firms that focus on executive searches, many of which are specialized by industry, far too expensive given that we were bootstrapping the company. Thus, we bumbled on our own, using a combination of the person's previous professional experience and our intuition about whether the person would fit into the culture to make our decisions. Too often the person I hired might have had many of the technical skills we needed but was either short on management skill or, more important, not sufficiently forceful to bring the kind of leadership we required. In retrospect, my judgment call about how the candidate would fit in with ETI's culture was frequently determined by whether I felt comfortable with the individual, and if I did, too often it was because I didn't feel threatened by the person's style and demeanor. More experienced and secure leaders don't feel threatened nor need to feel liked by the person they hire, and as a result, they are more likely to hire someone strong and let go of their power in that area.

## Letting Others Lead

Before letting go of some area and giving over full control of the day-to-day operation, I tend to spend a fair amount of one-on-one time with any new direct report until I feel comfortable that we have a common view of people's skills and the most important issues for which they are responsible. But I haven't appreciated that as I turn more decisionmaking over to other people, I also need to let go of my old ways of judging success and tracking the group's progress and the assumptions and tasks that once helped me be successful. In short, I needed a fresh perspective.

Sometimes, usually when you fail, you are forced into a new perspective. In chapter 8 we will discuss how failures offer great opportunities for growth. Ideally, however, many a failure could be avoided if the leader periodically withdrew and questioned even the most basic assumptions on which she has based her campaign.

## Stepping Down

Finally, all leaders eventually need to let go of the leadership role altogether. You may make this decision for different reasons. It may be that the troops have lost faith in you, that you have lost faith in yourself, that you are tired and cannot approach the role with the same level of energy that you once enjoyed, that you have failed and lost the war altogether, or that you have been wildly successful and know you were lucky. However, recognizing when to step aside is not easy for most leaders, in part because the very qualities required for successful leadership—persistence and courage—keep them focused in spite of setbacks and fear. Despite the exit and appearance of new lieutenants, if the group keeps falling short of its goals and for the same reasons, it is possible that some aspects of the war—*the market, the product, upper management, the revenue stream*—are ill-considered. The group may have good reasons to declare defeat and pack the tents, but it would be a bad end for a good leader to blame her defeat on external factors when it may be that she simply has exceeded her ability to grow and needs someone else to take over.

In his book *The Hero's Farewell: What Happens When CEOs Retire,* Jeffrey Sonnenfeld argues that the CEO is in many ways equivalent to a mythic hero that "battles beyond personal and historical limitations to a valid, human solution to the community's problems and conflicts."[5] Sonnenfeld explores how a number of successful CEOs have executed their retirement to the benefit or the detriment of their companies. Based on extensive interviews, he maintains that these executives can be placed in one of four groups:

> *Monarchs do not leave office until they are decisively forced out through the death of the chief executive or through an internal palace revolt. . . . Generals depart in a style also marked by forcible exit. Here, the chief executive leaves office reluctantly, but plots his return and quickly comes back to office out of retirement in order to rescue the company from the real or imaginary inadequacy of his successor. . . . Ambassadors, by contrast, leave office quite grace-*

*fully and frequently serve as post-retirement mentors. . . .
Governors rule for a limited time of office, then shift to
other vocational outlets entirely after retirement.*[6]

If power and position motivated a person to serve as a leader, he is more likely to respond like the monarch or the general. If he took on the role as a means of achieving some end, he is more likely to willingly transition to someone else at the appropriate time. In any case, everyone must step aside at some point regardless of their record of success. Thus, while you reassess the goals of your war and your group's progress in achieving them, you must look as clearly and critically at your own limitations as you do those of others.

## Notes

1. Unlike the poetic sagas that focused on dramatizing the histories of mythological figures, the family sagas sought to record the literal history of actual families and the seminal events in their lives.

2. *Njal's Saga,* translated by Magnus Magnusson and Hermann Pálsson (New York: Penguin, 1960), p. 135.

3. Cornelius Tacitus, *The Agricola and the Germania,* translated with an introduction by H. Mattingly, revised by S. A. Handford (New York: Penguin, 1970), pp. 112–133.

4. Mary Crawford Clawsey, "The *Comitatus* and Lord-Vassal Relationship in the Medieval Epic" (Ph.D. dissertation, University of Maryland, 1982), p. 24.

5. Jeffrey Sonnenfeld, *The Hero's Farewell: What Happens When CEOs Retire* (New York: Oxford University Press, 1988), p. 6.

6. Ibid., p. 70.

# Chapter 8

# Victory from Defeat
## Learning from Loss as a Precursor to Success

**B**elow is one of my favorite poems by e.e. cummings. It describes a man who could just never seem to get it right.

> nobody loses all the time
> i had an uncle named
> Sol who was born a failure and
> nearly everybody said he should have gone
> into vaudeville perhaps because my uncle Sol could
> sing McCann He Was a Diver on Xmas Eve like Hell
>     itself which
> may or may not account for the fact that my Uncle
>
> Sol indulged in that possibly most inexcusable
> of all to use a highfalootin phrase
> luxuries that is or to
> wit farming and be
> it needlessly
> added
>
> My Uncle Sol's farm
> failed because the chickens

*ate the vegetables so*
*my Uncle Sol had a*
*chicken farm till the*
*skunks ate the chickens when*
*my Uncle Sol*
*had a skunk farm but*
*the skunks caught cold and*
*died and so*
*my Uncle Sol imitated the*
*skunks in a subtle manner*

*or by drowning himself in the watertank*
*but somebody who'd given my Uncle Sol a Victor*
*Victrola and records while he lived presented to*
*him upon the auspicious occasion of his decease a*
*scrumptious not to mention splendiferous funeral*
       *with*
*tall boys in black gloves and flowers and everything*
       *and*
*i remember we all cried like the Missouri*
*when my Uncle Sol's coffin lurched because*
*somebody pressed a button*
*(and down went*
*my Uncle*
*Sol*

*and started a worm farm)*[1]

While few of us have Uncle Sol's bad luck, it is true that everybody eventually loses. Part of the reason I like early medieval Germanic and Celtic literature is that it presents this hard truth but never suggests that one shouldn't behave nobly in any case. As evidence, let's consider the poem *Beowulf.* For many years, most high school senior-year English texts included a translation of the first half of *Beowulf* as the first epic poem written in English. While the story was interesting enough, if a bit fanciful with its monster, Grendel, and his mother living at the bottom of a lake, it's just another heroic tale unless you read the entire poem.

In the first half Beowulf comes to Hrothgar, a chieftain of great renown whose hall is invaded every night by a horrific monster that is killing off his men. Promising his help, Beowulf successfully kills the monster and its mother to win great honor. Then in approximately one page, the poet recounts how Beowulf returns to Sweden, where he rules for twenty years until a slave in his kingdom steals a golden cup from a dragon's lair. The last half of the poem involves Beowulf setting out to kill the dragon, which had begun to attack his kingdom. Once again, Beowulf is successful, but this time he dies.

On the one hand, one could argue that Beowulf is killed in the battle simply because he is old and that the poet—or the shaper, who was writing a story that had been passed down orally for many generations—had no further intent. However, we can draw important parallels between the poem's first and second halves that suggest more is intended. In the first half, when Beowulf dives into Grendel's lake, his soldiers watch and fear the worst but remain in their places until Beowulf returns to the surface victorious. In the second half, there is almost an identical scene, where Beowulf's men wait outside the cave as he fights with the dragon. However, in this case, as time passes, they become convinced that he has been defeated, and all but one, Wiglaf, run away. (Recall that leaving the field when one's leader had been killed was one of the worst things a warrior could do in the comitatus tradition.) What, then, did the shaper intend with such a negative end to an otherwise heroic poem except to bring home the point that even the greatest of us are ultimately brought down in other's eyes, if not in our actual battles? In fact, looking at the cycle of the beatification and humiliation of "heroes" in today's popular press, one might argue that people have some innate need to discard their heroes in favor of someone new, if only so we never have to put ourselves at risk in supporting them.

In this chapter, we will examine why we fear failure and techniques for coping with our inevitable defeats, large or small, so that we can face losing and gain from it as well. In my experience, above and beyond the actual consequences, such as the loss of a job or worse, three primary areas of pain are associated with failure:

- shame for having disappointed your supporters and fear that they will think ill of you,

- sorrow that your supporters no longer have the same kind of faith in you, and

- disappointment in your own skills or performance.

In the following sections, we will examine each of these in turn, paying particular attention to areas where our own reaction is more intense than that of others since, as we have discovered elsewhere in the book, our emotional response usually masks some inner enemy that we must fight to move on.

## Shame about What Other People Think

All success—at least spiritual, if not material—depends on the courage to face risk. At the minimum, acknowledgment of our courage on the part of others, if not their active support and fealty, is one of the great rewards of success. Self-made men like Abraham Lincoln or such men as Nelson Mandela, who have conquered great odds and succeeded in making a difference, inspire our admiration and to a great extent, I believe, count others' appreciation as one of their greatest honors. As a result, when we fail or are discredited, we often feel shame that we have not proved to be as worthy as other people thought, and we dread what they must think of us now, grieving that we may be judged unworthy. While this reaction to failure is normal, we must consider several things when determining how important it is that we've disappointed others:

- the number of people affected and how dependent they are on you,

- the impact of your ability to perform your duties while moving forward, and

- the effect of vanity on your response.

## The Number of People Affected

How connected an individual feels to a particular group can greatly influence the way she sees the world and how seriously her failures will affect her. If she is part of a very prescriptive culture—for example, a member of a Southern Baptist, Amish, or Muslim community—she has been raised with a long list of rules governing what constitutes moral and acceptable behavior, including such issues as dancing, drinking alcohol, or using combustion engines. Cultures that are defined by such sets of edicts by definition constrain the types of risks individuals are allowed to take unless they are willing to leave the ranks of the faithful. If one goes outside the bounds of what's accepted, the results can be excommunication, exile, or worse, as in the case of Muslim communities, where honor killings still occur.

Most of us live under significantly fewer constraints, which allow us a greater range of risks and far less dramatic punishment in the case of failure. However, if we have visibly taken on some challenge and enjoyed the interest, if not support, of others in our community, one of the hardest things we must deal with after a failure is how it may affect our relationship with others. To some extent, this is a function of how much you care about other people and what they think.

I believe that most of us can divide the people we know

into three groups: people with whom you have a moral bond growing out of affection or duty or both, people to whom you have made a commitment, and people with whom you share no such bonds. The first group often includes customers, family and close friends, and individuals with whom you have struggled for some common cause. I consider the employees of ETI to be representative of the second group of people, or those to whom I have made a commitment as president of the company with respect to the company's vision, goals, and ethics. As for the last group, it may include people whom I find interesting and appealing, but with whom I have shared very little directly, aside from community board meetings, luncheons, and occasional cocktail parties.

When we suffer defeat or failure, we find ourselves worrying about all three sets of people but for different reasons. About the third class of people, or those who are not closely connected to the results of your efforts, you may worry about what they will think or say, but given that you have no obligation to them and that they will most likely be unaffected by your failure, you should care about their reactions least. And yet, for many, their concern—stemming possibly from either their imagination or their desire not to be judged unfairly—can be so vivid that it makes them want to withdraw from the community. Most of us recognize that we can be arch, if not downright cruel, in our assessment of other people, especially when we are around people we are comfortable with. When we fail and feel ashamed, then we imagine that the people who are not dependent on us are indulging in that same kind of small-minded gossip—we can almost hear their barbs—and they probably are gossiping, particularly if there has ever been any bad blood between you.

In my own case, I always imagine the worst for two reasons. First, over the years, particularly in my hotheaded, mouthing-off period, I offended many people and made an enemy or two. Even though I am now considerably more charitable to my fellow man and my subsequent manner and relative success have led to most people treating me with a semblance of good will, I recognize that some people would take pleasure in my bad fortune. The second reason that I suspect a number of people might take no small pleasure in my failure is that I am—and always have been—terrible at networking and at remembering the names and roles of people with whom I do not interact on a regular basis. As a result, it takes me far too long to acquire and remember their stories. Although I try to treat everybody I meet as if they were equally important, at some level I know I have unintentionally insulted people by not recognizing them or not being able to converse at great length about their accomplishments.

As hard as it is to endure our humiliation about what we (mostly) imagine that people are saying about us, it is even harder to feel that at some level we are being unfairly judged. Few people fail entirely on their own due to lack of skill or effort; it's usually a combination of factors, some of which are out of our control. Even the most self-critical person would like all the facts of his case to be known, but focusing on this aspect only makes him seem defensive.

In short, we have little control over what people think or say about us, particularly those with whom we do not share a bond. My approach for minimizing the importance or fears of what people think is to treat all public opinion—good and bad—as transitory and inaccurate, because to a large extent it always is. Whether you are being painted as a saint or a sinner, it's never the whole story. As a result, I have made it a practice not to read anything that has been written about me, even if it's good; I simply skim the article just to determine whether it is essentially positive or negative. This exercise has helped me in "not believing my press" so that when a negative article comes out, I don't torture myself about what was specifically said.[2] Finally, the best defense against bad publicity is to proceed as if nothing has happened. Without additional information, people who are not dependent on you soon grow tired of your story and move on to that of someone else.

## Loss of Faith

The response and feelings of people who are dependent on you—whether colleagues, employees, or customers—are significantly more important than generic public opinion. These people may have an imperfect knowledge of you as a person, but they count on you to deliver your end of a mutual commitment. When you fail these people—by missing a deadline, failing to meet the company's financial plan, or not providing them with the technical support they need to meet their own deadlines—they suffer the consequences. What these people think does matter, because frequently you are also dependent on them, and if they don't pick up the slack or stay committed to the cause, there will be further fallout. As a result, you must give them as accurate and straightforward a picture as possible, while asking them to keep faith with you.

The delicate balance here is where and how to place blame and to acknowledge fault. You should always be candid about mistakes in this type of relationship, because catching you in some untruth would be the quickest way for others to lose faith in you. The problem is that the most common cause of failure when at war in the workplace results from something you didn't know or something you failed to recognize, and admitting that shortsightedness is an invitation for others to judge you as not up to the task. For example, in the fall of 1996, after ETI had demonstrated four years of outstanding levels of growth and steady improvement toward profitability, we were ready to embark on the process of pursuing an initial public offering. Morale was great, although we heard some rumbling from one of the sales managers in North America. Unfortunately I did not pursue it after his manager assured me it was nothing. Four months into the process of working with the bankers, our chief financial officer registered concerns about our projections for the fourth quarter, which was usually our strongest. The numbers were far less than they should have been, which was not surprising when we realized that we were eight salespeople short of plan. So whose fault was this? The sales managers for not hiring to plan, the vice president of sales and the CFO for not tracking to this important number and voicing a concern, and mine for not managing the company with sufficient checks and balances in place to prevent this type of oversight. Postponing the IPO was extremely disappointing to everyone in the company, but we assured them that we would fix it. Unfortunately, the problem was worse than we knew. Not only were we short of plan, but most of the salespeople in North America had become disenchanted because they were focusing on lower-end prospects—which had neither the need nor the budget—rather than on the higher-end enterprise deals that helped the sales team in Europe grow by 98 percent the following year. As a result, a number of previously productive sales executives left, and we were forced to terminate several others who were not performing, as well as make a number of changes in sales management. Consequently, the turnaround that we hoped would happen in a period of nine to twelve months took more than two years, during which time many of our most experienced and talented technical people lost heart and left, discouraged that we seemed stuck in place while much newer *dot-com* companies were going public.

This period was very difficult for all of us and particularly for me. Like Penelope in *The Odyssey* at her tapestry,[3] I would regularly unravel the past to try to understand what threads I should have picked up on sooner and what structure and pattern we could put in place to prevent such surprises in the future. I also struggled with how to present it to the troops. Large hierarchical organizations can reorganize, using special assignments as a way of avoiding the public executions of managers who are being replaced, but we were too small to do this and valued our culture of interdependence too much to indulge in public floggings. As a result, I made a point of assuming as much of the responsibility for our shortcomings as anyone working for me.

While I believed I had the goodwill of most of the employees who had been with the company the longest—and who, because of our small size at the time of their hire, had worked more closely with me—like Beowulf, I wonder if they had lost faith in my skills and instincts to lead us to success. Fortunately, most of the managers who work directly for me are outstanding, and their continued commitment has helped keep us on course. Moreover, I decided that ETI needed a new hero for the troops to follow and accordingly promoted the individual who had been in charge of international to run worldwide sales and marketing. In addition to being extremely talented, Gérard Simon is charming and charismatic, and people are beginning to place more and more faith in him. Personally, this response has been gratifying because we need to recover our past momentum. Admittedly, however, I do have pangs that I receive less trust voicing the same opinion as Gérard. But ultimately, we should be joined in reaching a common goal, and the result is what's important.

Finally, those people who see your faults and recognize your shortcomings but remain steadfast in their support are your greatest gift. However, even though they are the most likely to forgive your shortcomings, their support does not relieve you of your obligation to remain committed to the values you have previously embraced and championed.

## Disappointment in Yourself

Other people's opinions aside, one of the hardest aspects of failure to face is not what others think about you, but what you fear about yourself. Most of us embrace our limitations as our own, but we believe that our successes are in good part due to luck. When we fail, then, we commonly want to treat the failure as symbolic, indicating that "the truth is finally out, and everyone will know that I am unworthy, or worse, a fraud." One of the hardest challenges we face when we fail is to acknowledge these feelings without being crippled by them. In the Catholic faith, suicide is a mortal sin because it means that you have judged the grace of God as being inadequate to save you. On a more secular note, if you focus only on your unworthiness after a failure, you are also guilty of despair.

The key is to face your weaknesses and inadequacies straight on and determine how you are either going to rectify your mistakes or, if that is not possible, change your behavior while moving forward. In earlier chapters, I recounted how I came to recognize that my outspoken, hostile, and judgmental attitude when dealing with others professionally made me many enemies. Only when this behavior led to my humiliation with the public cancellation of my research project was I motivated to change this behavior. Since that time I have made significant progress. I rarely lose my temper any more, and when I do, I am sick with regret for hours or days afterward. The rush of adrenaline that accompanies this outburst of fear—recall that anger is the mask of fear—almost makes me physically ill. I am still amazed that ten years ago I felt so much anger on a continual basis and felt revved up, almost like a car whose engine idles too fast.

I have made progress, but I have not yet conquered this problem. The year after we first encountered the problem with sales, I was far angrier than was effective. I have realized that part of what triggers this response is when I believe that people are not behaving in their own, much less the group's, best interest. For example, we used to have an alliance manager who, despite the fact that we were losing money doing business with X-Corp (in large part because they were not living up to their original commitment), would consistently give them even more of our scant resources rather than argue for greater equity.

**225**

Numerous times I asked him, publicly and privately, "Who is signing your check?" If I hadn't been so angry with myself over our general situation and frustrated, I might have found a better way to illustrate the problem so he could understand.

Defeat provides a wonderful opportunity for self-reflection and growth. However, like any important war, self-improvement requires more than one battle. At different points in my life, I have fought with some enemy, only to pull off her helmet and look into the eyes of a monster I thought I had defeated long ago. Her dress and manner may be different, but her intent is not. I used to find this pattern very discouraging until a friend of mine told me that I was using the wrong metaphor for progress. She said that because I used the metaphor of a line, when I passed point B and at some later time found myself back at that place, I thought I had lost ground. Her metaphor was that progress was like climbing along a spiral path out of a hole. As you progress, you often encounter the same point you had visited earlier, but at a different level. Progress involves acknowledgment and forgiveness. The spiritual path metaphor has helped me recognize when I have again indulged in old, unproductive ways and allowed me to focus at the same time on how I have progressed since the last time I visited that particular vice.

## Getting Over It

Nobody loses all the time. When you do fail, however, you must find a way to move on. With luck and introspection, this defeat might help you weaken one of your internal demons, but you must also deal with the external aspects of your defeat. The difficulty of this depends on the magnitude of the battle. Sometimes you can surrender and simply acknowledge that your behavior was destructive and then behave differently. In this case, if the victor is convinced that you have ceded your ground and will sincerely contribute toward the group's goal, there is a good chance that you can remain and thrive. At other times, you may need to pack up your tent and leave, as I left the CAD program at MCC after too much damage had been done. When leaving, you should also acknowledge your defeat, withdraw from the battle, and treat the victor with the respect he believes he deserves. Even if you liken him to the devil incarnate and feel he can't be trusted, your positive behavior will usually buy you time to retool or find another opportunity. Because few enemies—even the internal ones—are the devil incarnate, it also provides you with a chance to gain and give genuine respect and forgiveness.

If you use each defeat as an opportunity for growth, the battles over time become less personal, if necessary at all. And one day you will discover that although you have become a formidable warrior, you have chosen the path of the adventurer and would rather go around, under, through, or over the conflict and fight only when you have no other choice.

## Notes

1. e.e. cummings, *Poems 1923–1954* (New York: Harcourt, Brace and Company, 1954), pp. 173–74.

2. In the August 12, 1996, issue of *Forbes*, the cover story "How Katherine Hammer Reinvented Herself," painted me in a positive light, while the follow-up story "Back to the Books," which appeared in the September 20, 1999, issue, took an opposite position.

3. *The Odyssey* tells of the adventures of Odysseus in the seven years following the Trojan War. During that period, his home was in the charge of his wife, Penelope, and his son Telemachus. Assuming that Odysseus is dead, a group of young chieftains move in and demand that Penelope marry one of them. She puts them off for several years by saying that she must first complete weaving a shroud for her father-in-law by unweaving every night what she accomplished during the day.

# The Path to Peace

In this book, I have done my best to share with you the lessons of a poor horse, and in so doing, I have spent considerable time talking about how to deal with the negative emotions of fear and anger, and cope with weaknesses in ourselves and others. By examining these issues with me, I hope you have found the book to be encouraging; from every battle I've described, I have emerged stronger and more capable of joy. We all battle with our own limitations. The struggle between good and evil, light and dark, the saved and the damned, takes place in our hearts every day. Our real challenge is to conquer our shadow enemies—those that mask our fear and pain—so that regardless of our success in the battles we wage in the workplace, we move forward with greater serenity and satisfaction.

# index